Vision
Courage
& Heart

Visual Leaders Press
800 Wildwood Drive
Charleston, WV 25302

Library of Congress Cataloging-in-Publication Data

Robert G. Lynn, 1932 -
Vision Courage & Heart: Lessons in leadership from author Bob Lynn,
who used uncommon common sense to lead two newspapers to photojournalism greatness
1. Photojournalism 2. Leadership 3. Management

Library of Congress Control Number: 2013932743

Design by Kevin Dilley

Photos used in this book with permission of the following copyright hold-
ers: The Virginian Pilot/Landmark Media Enterprises LLC; The Charleston Gazette/The Daily Gazette Company; June Morgan; and Michelle
Frankfurter.

ISBN: 978-0-9888443-0-8

Printed in the USA by Merrick Industries

boblynnvisioncourageandheart.com

ON THE COVER   This picture of Tiny Buck, a 16-year-old who had just received a new
heart, epitomizes the power of documentary visual journalism, says author Bob Lynn. The
photo connects with viewers because of the story it tells by simultaneously capturing
Tiny's fear and the loving concern of those around her. The image was made by Virginian-Pilot
photographer Motoya Nakamura.

AND MY VERY SPECIAL THANKS TO:

My wife Millie and sister Jane Lynn, for their excellent editing help ... Rob Kinmonth and Bill Ballenberg for helping me get the book started in the right direction ... Jennifer Boucher Albers of Creative Circle Media Consulting for her initial design work ... and daughter-in-law Chana Lynn for developing and maintaining the book's Web site, BobLynnVisionCourageandHeart.com.

My special thanks also to Stacie Chandler and Fran Ostendorf for copyediting the book.

Finally, I want to offer my undying gratitude to three incredible friends who made Vision, Courage and Heart possible through their efforts and enthusiastic, never-ending belief in the book. They are Bill Ostendorf, president and CEO of Creative Circle, who contributed his company's resources and his personal expertise; Curt Chandler, my content editor who struggled with me over every word and picture; and Kevin Dilley, who designed the book.

~ Bob Lynn

CONTENTS

How do you measure a person's impact on an industry when his genius is in leading people, molding them into a team that produces a truly exceptional visually driven newspaper, day after day, year after year?

Contests are one yardstick. His paper dominated the National Press Photographers Association quarterly picture editing clip contest for years. The NPPA and the Society of News Design repeatedly recognized the paper for best use of photography. Impressive awards indeed, but they still fall short of recognizing the scale of this editor's accomplishments. That's because Bob Lynn led not one, but two newspapers to visual excellence. Along the way he created a culture that helped one newspaper in particular – The Virginian-Pilot in Norfolk – to sustain that level of excellence not only while he was there, but for more than a decade (and counting) after he retired. His legacy extends from coast to coast, where his former employees are making other newspapers better by applying the photographic and leadership skills they learned at the Virginian-Pilot.

Perhaps the best way to measure the impact Bob Lynn has had on the newspaper industry is in the words of his co-workers, competitors, former employees and mentors. Their thoughts capture the qualities that make Bob's lessons important not only for future visual editors, but for managers in any field charged with harnessing the talents of creative people:

"What Bob provided was a kind of soil where I could grow myself completely and utterly in a way that I had never experienced before. The environment that he created was incredible – a photographer's dream! I was in this really charged up environment that was all about excellence and risk taking and – yes! – fun. Up until then I always felt like my hands were tied, that I had to adapt to someone else's ideas. But Bob just untied my hands the minute I got there. It was like he freed me up. He did it with a lot of love. I know it's funny to talk about love in this context, but it's true. It was such a special time. Those years formed so much of who I am and I treasure them.

- Beth Bergman Nakamura
Hired by Bob as a Virginian-Pilot photographer
Now at The (Portland) Oregonian

"Bob Lynn was my boss for 10 years. He knew when to challenge me in a positive way and he knew when to stand back and let me do the best job I knew how. We formed a management team that achieved excellence we could feel each day. The atmosphere at the paper was not always bliss, but with Bob's support, my feeling was we could work out any difficulty. I will always remember this era at The Virginian-Pilot as one of the best in my working life.

- Alex Burrows
Hired by Bob as a Virginian-Pilot picture editor
Retired in June 2007 as director of photography

"Bob Lynn was a great boss. He hired the best creative people to do the work. He always encouraged risk-taking. He inspired people to be understanding and considerate of one another. And he always stepped in quickly when problems arose. He never raised his voice or showed anger. The Virginian-Pilot's reputation as a great paper where people truly care about each other is his enduring legacy.

- Sam Hundley
Artist, projects designer and illustrator, The Virginian-Pilot
Hired by Bob twice, in 1984 and 1994

"Bob Lynn hired me 30 years ago for my first job in photojournalism. My first day was because of another photographer's last day. When Bob took over at the Charleston Gazette, one of the staffers he inherited was Lew Raines, an older photographer with limited ability. Bob could ask the paper to fire Lew, or he could spend a great deal of time bringing Lew's skills up to par. He chose the latter. Bob tells Lew's story in Chapter Five of this book. There is a lesson in that story — how you treat people. It is a lesson Bob taught me, one that stays with me to this day. Bob did the right thing. He always has.

- Randy Olson
National Geographic magazine photographer
Bob's second hire at the Charleston (W.Va.) Gazette

"With the help of Ohio University photojournalism professor Chuck Scott, I persuaded Bob Lynn to move from his home state of West Virginia to Norfolk. He was urgently needed at the Virginian-Pilot. Photo assignments were being shot by a veteran, dispirited staff. Pictures were being edited by editors who lacked talent and training in visual journalism. Progress was rapid and Bob's personal job skills were important in the transformation that followed. Yet I believe the decisive ingredient was his leadership ability. He found more talent in the existing photo staff than any of us would have predicted. Talented photographers and editors from elsewhere proved eager to work for and with Bob. Technical skill alone could never have achieved so much.

- Frank Caperton
Former executive editor of The Virginian-Pilot
Retired editor of the Indianapolis Star

"Bob's early work as a reporter who made pictures at The Los Angeles Times and the Cincinnati Enquirer helped bridge the chasm between word and picture people. Playing both fiddles gave him a perspective few photographers share and paid off with enhanced credibility in his work as a picture editor. Later his dedication to photojournalism was tested when he drove 300 miles roundtrip from Cincinnati to Athens twice a week to attend 8 a.m. graduate classes at Ohio University. After driving back to Cincinnati, he worked the night shift. Bob's masterful ability to hyper-motivate photographers and influence editors paid off in Charleston and Norfolk. His ambition, intuitiveness, imagination, enthusiasm, inspiration, leadership and hard work built photo operations of distinction.

As we say down home, he done good.

- Chuck Scott
Founder and director emeritus,
School of Visual Communication, Ohio University

"When Bob came to Norfolk I was apprehensive and also determined not to get lost in the shuffle ... I thank Bob Lynn for the years

I was able to spend as one of his photographers. His patience with me and my quick temper taught me some self-control. His fairness in giving everyone a chance also served me well in the end. I have come to believe he was the best boss I ever worked for.

- Robie Ray
Long-time Virginian-Pilot photographer, now retired

66 Never before or since have I worked with someone so dedicated to pictures and their powers to tell a story. Bob's approach to photojournalism has always been to strip away the excess and get to the heart of the matter. He wanted me, and all his photographers, to grow as photojournalists but, more importantly, as people.

- Lawrence Jackson
White House photographer, Washington, D.C.
Hired by Bob as a Virginian-Pilot photographer

66 I have often felt that the media, because of space constrictions and reader preferences, inhibit creativity. Bob Lynn refused to be inhibited. Not only did he challenge his newspaper editors and readers with bright, daring photos and news accounts, but he excited them. Read his message. It is not just for yesterday, but for use every day.

- Leo Chabot
Former chief photographer of the Charleston Gazette
and retired Sunday editor of The Lawrence (Mass.) Eagle-Tribune

66 The lesson I learned from Bob, and what I think about even when dealing with my children, is everyone has the potential to succeed given the right encouragement and support. Bob just assumed everyone would do well and he was rarely disappointed. He's a carrot, not a stick, kind of boss. And we all loved him for it. He was the type of boss one could argue with strongly, but he never held it against you. He backed his shooters 100 percent, in the field, as well as in the newsroom. We weren't only photographers, we were also journalists. Bob treated us the way he treated his family, with respect, giving fatherly advice, pride in what we did and encouragement when things got rough. We loved him for it. Twenty years later, the Virginian-Pilot photographic family still gets together for reunions, and each time, it's like we've never been apart.

- Karen Kasmauski
Former staff photographer at The Virginian-Pilot
Long-time National Geographic photographer

Bob Lynn is retired from The Virginian-Pilot, but his expertise remains very much in demand. He taught photojournalism for several semesters at Syracuse University, including a term in London. He has consulted at newspapers and conducted workshops in Australia, Singapore and across the United States.

He has always been a master at balancing life and work. Bob devotes a considerable amount of time to family and friends; he is retired, after all. Fortunately for the industry he never quite left, Bob has also been finding time to write this book.

Editing Vision, Courage & Heart has been a personal learning experience. I consider myself a reasonably successful visual leader. While I was director of photography at the Pittsburgh Post-Gazette we received our fair share of recognition, including national awards for picture editing and photo usage. Staff photographer Martha Rial won the Pulitzer Prize for news photography. But looking back now, I realize how much better we could have been if I'd read this book before I took that job, instead of after I left the newspaper to teach at Penn State. My loss is your gain, because now you have Bob's book in your hands.

Start reading!

- Curt Chandler

What you'll learn in this book
and some thoughts about the future

Leadership

This book is about becoming an outstanding leader. About excelling possibly far beyond your wildest dreams.

It is a book for anyone who is a manager, or hopes to be a manager some day, who is determined to excel in their field. It is a book drawn from my experiences at two newspapers, but I think you will find that the lessons in each story universally ring true — lessons about creating an exceptionally high quality, productive work environment. It is a book for those desiring to lead their operations to much greater heights.

Thus, this book is not an academic discussion about visual journalism. It is not about theory. This book is just me talking to you – about how I and a bunch of other photojournalists helped pull two American newspapers (The Gazette in Charleston, W.Va., and The Virginian-Pilot in Norfolk, Va.) out of a visual Dark Age to light up the newspaper photojournalism skies.

In this book, you'll learn how we built great photo staffs that produced exceptional pictures. You'll learn how we got those exceptional photos into the newspaper every day, not just occasionally. You'll learn about the philosophy I brought to the job as leader/manager, the philosophy that I believe was the heart and soul of our successes. You'll learn about the many practical things I did to bring out the best in people, common sense things that might be better described as un-common common sense. You'll learn about vision, truly understanding your job and the critical importance of positive motivation.

I'll talk a lot about motivation. You'll learn about the vital connection between motivation and great picture content. And you'll learn about many other areas where motivation comes into play.

And you'll learn that, when it comes to hiring people, thinking creatively can help build a great staff. When it comes right down to it, it's all about people – and motivating those people to perform at their highest potential.

The future — Core mission won't change

As I write this book, the news industry is going through revolutionary change. Newspapers are facing the toughest challenge in their long history — an audience shift to online news is luring both the young and not-so-young to its 24-hour text and visual news reports from seemingly endless sources.

Newspapers have established their own Web sites, drawing audience, but not nearly the same amount of revenue as print. As online technology zips us further into the new age, how will it affect the way we do our jobs? Photographers, reporters, word editors and picture editors are already working together in new ways to tell stories with still images, video and sound. Who knows what else the future may demand?

Whether our pictures are delivered on the printed page or via Internet, there are two things that will not change:

• First, our core mission to deliver to our readers the most effective and highest quality news content, in pictures and words.

• Second, the need for your inspirational leadership to motivate your staff to perform at its highest possible level.

My hope is that this book, in combination with your natural talents and strengths, will give you the knowledge, insight and courage to perform at your most inspired level as a leader and manager in our evolving news business.

~ Bob Lynn

EDITOR'S NOTES

About the pictures in this book

The images that appear at the beginning of each chapter are examples of the artistic, risk-taking and storytelling photography that Bob Lynn expected and inspired. Most were made by staff photographers at the Virginian-Pilot. Of the remaining pictures, one was made by freelance photographer Michelle Frankfurter for the Pilot. The others were made by Randy Olson and Bill Kelley III when they worked for Bob at The Charleston Gazette.

Bob offers a lesson in each caption.

Newspaper names

When Bob started his 17-year career in Norfolk, he was director of photography for Landmark Communication's editorially independent morning Virginian-Pilot and afternoon Ledger-Star. Two years later the papers merged with both names appearing on the masthead. The name of the combined paper was finally shortened to The Virginian-Pilot. For brevity's sake, in most cases, Bob uses only The Virginian-Pilot name.

Vision & Philosophy

The path to photo greatness

1 THE VISION

Voices

It started with the voices.

Voices in my head about running a photo department.

Yet the last thing I wanted to do was be a manager. I was a staff photographer at the Cincinnati Enquirer. Hey, I loved shooting pictures for a living. And besides, I'd seen so many negative management styles in my career, I had no desire to join the club.

But the voices persisted. Actually, it was more my brain having a conversation with itself – "You know ... if ever I was in charge of a newspaper photo operation, I'd do it differently." All kinds of ideas poured through my head about ways I'd lead and manage.

I knew that newspapers where I had worked – as well as others across the country – could be much better. Could give their readers much more. Better pictures. Better use of pictures. Better-designed pages. It was clear that at most newspapers, man-

HOMELESS Documentary photography is the heart and soul of what we should be doing as newspaper photojournalists. These homeless children sleep where they can – tents, shelters, motels and here in a car. Jamie Francis

agement's low expectation for photo content had become self-fulfilling prophecy. The photo department was seen as strictly a service department, not as a professional, creative group of people capable of producing superior, storytelling work.

Bends of the visual deep

And, unfortunately, the same is still true today. Photographers and picture editors at many newspapers suffer from what I would call "the bends of the visual deep." They've had their enthusiasm and caring for photography driven out of them by an indifferent tradition-bound newsroom culture, a culture that still regards photos as window dressing for the printed page or fodder to feed the Web site. Worn down, the photographers and picture editors have simply given up hope.

Sadly, in many cases, the same can be said for photo department managers. Some, I'm sure, are not even aware that they have – for all practical purpose – hoisted the white flag of surrender.

These long-suffering members of the photo department simply put up with:

- Not being included in story planning.
- Poorly conceived photo requests.
- Unnecessary last-minute assignments.
- Too many assignments in a day (meaning photographers don't have time to produce quality work).
- Being told exactly what and how to shoot assignments by people who don't leave the newsroom.
- Having to turn in virtually "everything shot" (as in, "we don't trust the photographer or picture editors to make good choices").
- Not having the best and most compelling pictures used.
- Having pictures poorly cropped, sized and displayed.

And upper management typically doesn't have a clue. "Hey, it's your job. You're getting paid. What's the complaint?"

Where's the content?

And that's only the half of it. There are newspapers out there doing a decent job with pictures. Decent content. Maybe good, or even strong, photo use. I figure people at these papers are pretty much satisfied. I don't want to be a killjoy here, but they shouldn't be. They may be doing a superior job with picture selection and use, but there is an ugly little truth about content in American newspapers today. Even the good ones fall short a lot. Day in, day out, picture content isn't nearly what it could be, or should be.

It doesn't have to be that way. We can do better.

The voices kept ringing in my ears with ideas about managing a photo operation. Slowly I came around from "if I was ever in charge" to "I want to be in charge." I thought – "I can do this. I can make a difference. I can work with photographers, picture editors – and everyone else in the building – reporters, word editors, designers, production people. We can all be successful."

The vision

It was clear to me what needed to be done. First, set photographic content standards high – even the sky should be no limit. In other words, a staff producing only ordinary "good" photography would not do. Second, build an outstanding photo staff. One where everyone fulfills her or his potential. Third, produce a great daily photo report that is used effectively. One that is great, not once in a while, but every day.

And never forget that, in the end, it's all about quality photographic content and serving the reader.

That's it. It's that simple. Set high standards. Build a great staff. And know that your No. 1 job is – day in, day out – seeing to it that your staff produces an exceptional photo report. That it produces pictures better than anything the editors, reporters, designers and readers have ever seen. Pictures so exceptional that they will make their own case for being used effectively.

No. 1 job

It seems to me that many photo managers never stop to think that their No. 1 responsibility is the day in, day out production of an outstanding daily photo report. They're consumed with simply getting all the photo assignments covered, or obtaining new equipment, or balancing the budget, or putting all of their energy into photo projects, or just pleasing the boss. While all are important in their own way, they are not your No. 1 job.

There is really no excuse if all you have to offer readers on a daily basis is boring, cliché images. For those photo managers who don't put the photo report first, it's a case of not seeing the forest for the trees. If your paper isn't producing excellent pictures every day and running them well, then what's the point of your job? If the paper's design sucks, campaign for a better design. If you have the skill, maybe redesign the paper yourself. And if picture reproduction on the presses is out of register half of the time, work with the press crews to change that.

The voices and common sense

So, lo and behold, I had a vision. I had a mission. I knew I wanted to run a photo department. And I could hear the voices, over and over again, telling me how to lead a staff to greatness, that the most important things to remember were really just common sense things – kinda Sunday School stuff.

- Treat every staff member like you would like to be treated.
- Believe in them and they will believe in themselves.
- Respect them and they will respect themselves, and their self-confidence will grow.
- Trust your staffers and they will be trustworthy.
- Treat them fairly because it's the right thing to do, as well as the smart thing to do.
- Use lots and lots of positive reinforcement.
- Be absolutely honest with them, but always leave them their dignity and dreams.
- Have an open-door policy that is really open. Welcome suggestions, welcome criticism.
- Never assume someone's guilt without knowing the facts (know the deep wounds that come from being falsely accused).
- Reward excellence.
- Hire people who are not only bright, talented, full of energy and passionate about photojournalism, but who are of "good heart," meaning they care about other people.

Motivation – the bricks and mortar of success

When you add up all these common sense (or better put, un-common common sense) or feel good ways to work with your staff, it points to one thing – MOTIVATION.

Motivation is the bricks and mortar for building a successful – let's make that a great – photo operation.

And so, when I took the plunge into the deep waters of leader-ship and management at The Charleston Gazette (three years) and at The Virginian-Pilot (17 years), all the things the voices had been telling me – all of them – proved for me to be the Holy Grail of leading and managing a photo department. What we were able to accomplish at those two newspapers was like magic, so reward-ing and so darn much fun.

2 WHAT IT TAKES

Believe in yourself

Leading a photo operation to its full potential – are you ready for the challenge? Of course, none of us knows until we've been tested by that challenge. But there are character traits, personality makeup, personal convictions and skills that will be key to your success.

One is an absolute must. That is a strong belief in yourself. It's not that you go around thinking you're hot stuff. But you do have confidence in yourself. You know who you are and it feels comfortable.

You enjoy working with people. You stand up for yourself and for what you believe. You are honest and straightforward. You care about and help others in such a way that they will be inspired to also care about and help others. You don't put others down

---

BODY WORKS Body language and "the moment" make a strong combination in this photograph of two USS George Washington carrier crewmen exchanging greetings as they rotate their duty watch. **Bill Tiernan**

– those on the photo staff or people in the newsroom. You are a person who stays calm, cool and collected (not that you can't show that you feel strongly about some things). You're not afraid to take risks. In other words, you have confidence in yourself.

A staff's worst nightmare

It has always struck me that managers who lack self-confidence often come across as macho, overbearing and supposedly totally in control (and don't listen to their staff). They are, in truth, holding up a mask, creating a defensive barrier. They feel other people are surely out to take advantage of them, so not trusting other people (which also can mean not taking risks) becomes a part of their defense and part of their management style. They cover their asses. They turn people off. They are a staff's worst nightmare.

Simply put, to be a truly successful leader you must have the

---

WHAT TO DO BEFORE YOU BECOME THE BOSS

If you think you want to lead a photo department at some point, but aren't sure you are ready for such a challenge, there are things you can do to prepare yourself.

If you are a photographer, get into the newsroom. Talk to reporters, word editors and picture editors about potential stories to be photographed. Talk to them about the paper's news coverage in general. Listen and learn the inner workings of the newsroom and the newspaper overall. The main thing is, work hard to become respected in the newsroom.

If you are a picture editor, you are already "in training" to become the leader of a photo operation. And, hopefully, you are learning through experience some of the do's and don'ts of what it takes to become a successful leader.

Whether you are a photographer or a picture editor, talk to people in the newsroom about ways the newspaper might improve itself, visually and otherwise. Don't be afraid to express your views to the paper's top editors. Be willing to take risks.

As you become a successful contributor in the newsroom, your confidence and belief in yourself will grow, as will your ability to teach and lead others.

courage to believe in yourself, which in turn will give you the courage to believe in each person on your staff. That belief will be your most powerful means of inspiring each and every photographer and picture editor to believe in themselves. And, miracle of miracles, the photo operation successes will burst forth like flowers in spring. As that happens, it will create a self-perpetuating energy. Performance will improve. Everyone's belief in themselves (self-esteem) will grow. And thus, onward and upward.

The stuff of dreams

Of course, no photo leader is a perfect Super Hero, but if there ever is one it will be a person who:

- Has VISION to see a better photo world.
- Is a true LEADER who inspires others to perform at their best.
- Is a dedicated, passionate and skilled journalist who loves and knows the news; and shows excellent news judgment.
- Is a dedicated, passionate and skilled photojournalist who loves, knows and believes in the communicative power of pictures – and how to marry pictures with good design.
- Has extremely high picture quality/content standards.
- Knows that the No.1 job is to produce great pictures every day and see to it that they are run effectively.
- Has a people-oriented philosophy and management style; is a coach, a teacher, a motivator; understands the power of positive reinforcement.
- Treats staff members as she or he personally would want to be treated. Believes in each one of them.
- Is a self-starter, has drive, is a can-do person, is energetic and enthusiastic.
- Has the courage, and guts if you will, to fight for what is right; does not duck tough, unpleasant situations; takes care of problems NOW, but knows when not to get involved.
- Is a good communicator. Can articulate his or her ideas and beliefs to convince others to see their merits.
- Is accessible, a good listener. Encourages suggestions. Can take criticism. Leaves ego at the door.
- Has patience.
- Respects and cares about staff (professionally and personally).
- Is a team player, a team builder.

- Is a person of "good heart." Is compassionate.
- Is perceptive.
- Is fair. Is absolutely honest, but always leaves staffers with their dignity and dreams.
- Rewards excellence.
- Has good organizational skills.
- Is a problem solver who isn't afraid to make a decision; who isn't afraid to fail as long as a lesson can be learned from the failure.
- Knows when to delegate responsibility.
- Respects others even if they hold opposing views. Is strong willed, but can compromise.
- Is a creative thinker, can "think out of the box." Is willing to take risks with pictures and people.
- Encourages the staff to take chances.
- Has a sense of humor and encourages the staff to have fun.

Resolve, hard work and believing

No one has it all. The challenge is for you to work on the areas you feel need improvement. That goes for all of us. Don't be discouraged.

So, leading a photo operation to greatness isn't easy. It takes a lot of resolve and hard work. But in the end, I believe it is all worthwhile – the production of exceptional storytelling photography on a daily basis and the personal satisfaction of bringing that photography to light.

But most important of all is believing in yourself and in others. If you do, I believe you will be well on your way to becoming a successful leader.

3 NOT YOUR USUAL START

Vision from above

I got my first hint that things in Norfolk could be special the day Virginian-Pilot Executive Editor Frank Caperton picked me up at the airport for the director of photography job interview.

At the time I was the graphics editor of the Charleston Gazette, my first management job. I loved working in my hometown, but money was a bit tight in West Virginia when it came to supporting a family of five. And Frank Caperton was talking about a $10,000 a year raise, plus he said he was recruiting me to turn the Pilot's photographic fortunes around, as I had done with the Gazette.

So there I was being picked up at the Norfolk airport by the Virginian-Pilot's top editor. Even more interesting was that we did not go back to the newspaper. For the next five hours – in a hotel room Frank had reserved for the day – we exchanged ideas about newspapering, in general, and the role of photography in the newsroom, in particular. Now here was my kind of editor, an original and unconventional thinker.

GOOD SEEING Bill Kelley, freelancing for the Charleston Gazette, avoids a cliché band picture by showing a good eye for humor. **Bill Kelley III**

We discussed, philosophized and mused about photo content, management styles, upper management support, our personal goals for the newspaper and everything photojournalistic we could think of. He interviewed me. I interviewed him. It went well. We were on the same page.

Frank words

As we crossed the hotel parking lot to Frank's car, before heading to the newspaper, I found myself saying, "Frank, I want you to know something. If you end up offering me the job, I want you to know that the first person I will try to please will not be you. It will be me. But I hope that in pleasing myself, you, too, will be pleased."

I've thought back many times on this parking lot statement. It came out of the blue, but I came to understand that these were words of wisdom with a powerful connection to accomplishing something special, something unique.

In effect, I was saying to Frank, if you hire me ... hire me for my vision, my philosophy, my leadership and management style, my experience and for who I am. Then stand back and let's see if what I do works for you.

Another point to be made here is that, in order to achieve great results, I'm convinced that a leader must be ready and willing to lose his or her job if they are going to truly do a job at the highest level. Be willing to take chances, willing to buck old systems. You cannot achieve excellence if your primary goal is simply to hang onto your job.

"Tell me what to do, boss, I'm good at following orders," will, in all likelihood, only lead to mediocrity.

Think of people in history (explorers, inventors, medical researchers, pioneers, business people) who accomplished great things. Almost every one of them had their own vision and, with dogged purpose, pursued that vision – their way. They were able to convince others – through persuasion or deed – to embrace that vision.

The first key to unlocking the door to success is vision and the courage to believe fully in that vision.

Yes, if you fail (and failure is always possible) the newspaper may ask you to step down, or even hit the road. But if you're willing to live by your vision, greatness is possible.

It's your call.

4 CHOOSING THE RIGHT BOSS

Beware of the Tower of Babel

Imagine you're facing a career decision. The question is: should you take the job? You're interviewing for the head photographic position (or perhaps a combination photographic and design position). You've laid out your vision to top management of what you hope to accomplish.

Those managers, including the one who will be your immediate boss, say they are on board with your vision. They say they want you to visually take the paper to a new level. That's why they've offered you the job.

So it's decision time. You know that doing the job successfully will take a lot of hard work. Along with many other things, it's also going to take good people skills and a strong will on your

---

SURPRISE When a wave of FA-18 fighter jets came screaming in from an unannounced direction, during a Navy air show, quick and creative thinking resulted in this striking image of the jets and Green Run High School ROTC student James Terry. **Nhat Meyer**

part. But one of the most important ingredients in the formula for success is the strong backing of upper management. The time to determine if that backing will be there is when you are interviewing. (Note: You are interviewing management, just as they are interviewing you.)

During the interviewing process you may think that you and the paper's top editors are talking the same language, but in fact you may not be. Assume nothing. Beyond talking about your photographic vision for the newspaper, make sure they truly understand your vision and the kinds of changes you foresee such as:

- You and the photo department will have control over what photo requests will be assigned.
- No more check-passing and plaque presentation pictures.
- There will be better use of pictures in general, but particularly on section fronts.
- The photo department will turn in its best pictures, not every picture.

It's one thing for a managing editor and other editors to say you'll have their backing, but the trick is to figure out if they have the guts to stand by their promises. When you begin to recommend changes, will they support your ideas in the face of inevitable opposition from some people in the newsroom? Who will the top editors go with? You, the new visual leader, or other editors and staffers (some who may be longtime friends of the top editors)?

How do you determine if your prospective boss and other key managers will stick to their words? While interviewing, ask for an opportunity to talk with staff members – photographers, reporters, designers, middle level editors. If you get a sense there is mutual respect and trust between the staff and management, that's a good sign.

If not, be warned. There are newspapers out there that have an ongoing culture of shark-infested waters when it comes to how top managers deal with each other and the staff.

Of course, there is no sure-fire way to know if the top editors will give you the backing that you will need. In the end, you will have to call on your ability to read people and your gut instincts.

We stink. You fix it

When Charleston Gazette Editor Don Marsh hired me, he told me he knew nothing about photography or newspaper design, but he had a strong opinion concerning both at the Gazette. "We stink. You fix it," he charged, "and I'll back you up."

I had a strong sense he would do just that. And he did.

Changes came pretty quickly and easily with the photo operation. But making layout and design changes was another matter.

When I arrived at the Gazette, it was one of the ugliest newspapers in the country. Garish tint blocks – some dark red, some bright yellow – were eyesores that regularly pocked the front page. Stories were jammed into this shape and that on the pages. Pictures, mostly routine in nature, were run small and in awkward arrangements.

To begin to address these design problems, I ordered two Gazettes to be delivered to our home each day (one for the family, one for me). As soon as I got up in the morning, I grabbed one of the papers and a red China marker and began identifying visual potholes.

At the paper, I worked with Executive Editor Tex Higbee, the paper's most astute editor when it came to visuals. But it was the chief copy editor and his layout crew who were responsible for getting out the paper each night. And they bristled at being asked to accept a world of new layout concepts and a higher respect for photography.

Eyes narrowed. Sarcasm wasn't unheard of.

"It's either Lynn or me"

Of course, it is human nature to resist change. Most people would rather keep doing things the old way. The chief copy editor was no exception. He regularly charged into Don Marsh's office to complain about the new graphics editor and his newfangled design ideas.

One day he'd had enough. He stormed into Marsh's office and announced, "It's either Lynn or me." Marsh looked up at his red-faced copy chief and said, "Well ... Bob Lynn isn't going anywhere."

That's the kind of backing I'm talking about.

In a crowded room

Another example of the kind of backing it takes to bring about change took place soon after I arrived in Norfolk. I had just hired the Pilot's first-ever picture editor, Roman Lyskowski, a talented Pilot staff photographer skilled in design. Executive Editor Frank Caperton called a meeting of the Pilot newsroom editors.

Caperton, the editors, Roman and I crowded into a conference room. Caperton introduced Roman as the paper's new (and first) picture editor. He said that Roman was being given this responsibility because of his newspaper experience and visual expertise. Caperton said it would be Roman's job to select and crop pictures and recommend their display.

Caperton said that, on any given night, when it came to making the final decision on what picture would run, say, as the lead on page one, the final call would not go to Roman, but to the person in charge of the newsroom that night, the news editor.

He went on to say, however, "But if the news editor decides to not follow Roman's recommendation, the next morning he had better have a damn good reason."

Even though Caperton said that, it didn't follow that Roman was immediately accepted with open arms into the Pilot newsroom. One tough veteran editor – in fact, the news editor himself – admitted to me later that he started out with a decidedly negative attitude about Roman. He recalled thinking, "Why should this young punk photographer be telling me what pictures to run, a job I've been doing for 20 years?" But after a month or so, he said his attitude about Roman had changed to "Where's Roman? We need Roman in on this. What does Roman think?"

Passport to success

The beautiful part of this story is that Caperton didn't try to stuff Roman Lyskowski down the newsroom's throat. He knew that Roman would have to win over the word editors through his diplomatic skills and by showing how much he could help them with pictures. But it was through his backing that Caperton handed Roman his passport to success.

It was the same passport he handed me when I first arrived on the job. When he introduced me to both newsrooms (back when the Pilot was two newspapers) he did not dictate that I had absolute power over what pictures ran in the papers or how they were to be used. He said the newspapers' new goals when it came to photography were the creation of superior pictures and using them in a sophisticated, compelling manner – and that I was hired to lead the way in fulfilling those goals.

Caperton (whom I consider the Godfather of the Norfolk photo revolution) backed the changes all the way, never wavering. He was a man of his word. It is not surprising. Prior to my arrival in Norfolk, he had picked the brains of some of the most gifted and knowledgeable photojournalism leaders in the country to find out how to bring photo excellence to the Pilot. He listened, learned and went into action. His message was clear – we need to change, we must change, we will change. The pressure was on. Those in the newsroom got the message – some more quickly than others – but the road to success had been cleared.

Don't underestimate how important this backing is. It can be the difference between success and failure, joy and despair.

So, ultimately, you have to decide if upper management and your potential boss are people you can comfortably work with and who will faithfully support you and your vision.

If the answer is "yes," then go for it.

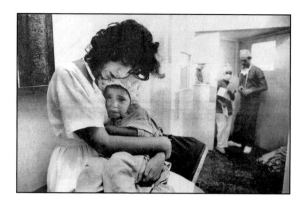

5 YOU GOTTA BELIEVE

Lew's story

Lew Raines was a large beefy man, more than six feet tall. Really a bear of a man. He had done some boxing in his younger days and looked it. Most people wouldn't have guessed he was a newspaper photographer. When I took over as the Charleston Gazette's first graphics editor, Lew had been at the paper for many years.

I found there was virtually no respect in the newsroom for Lew or the other three Gazette photographers. Oh, they were thought of as nice enough fellows, but competent newspaper photographers ... no. And Lew was at the bottom of this second-class totem pole.

Which meant that morale in the photo department was lower than a West Virginia rattlesnake's belly. So, it was do your job, get no respect, go home, forget it. And the fact was, Lew and the other three photographers were indeed underperforming. But I

OPERATION HONDURAS It's documentary pictures like this of Emma Maricela Caceres being held by nurse Velvalens Ives of Norfolk that make an emotional connection with the reader. Bill Ballenberg

thought to myself, no wonder, after years of receiving negative comments and little encouragement, the expectations had become reality.

The truth was, all of these guys had become newspaper photographers because they loved photography, just like most newspaper photographers across the country. But slowly, over time, they had withdrawn into a corner of numbed indifference.

"Okay guys, this is a new day," I said to them when I took over at the Gazette. "Everyone is starting out with a clean slate." I told them I knew they had talent. I knew they were willing to work hard and knew they were going to produce some outstanding pictures. And they did.

But for Lew, a man who took life on with pessimistic comic good humor, the new day came slowly. I believed in Lew. I spent a lot of time working with him, using lots of positive reinforcement. Lew was easy to work with. Despite his bear-like presence, he was, by nature, a gentle man.

He took constructive criticism well. We worked and worked together. Assignment after assignment. I coached, suggested and looked over every frame. I let him know his images were getting better, telling the stories better. He was becoming enthusiastic. Happy.

One day he came back from an assignment with a lovely set of pictures of a mother working on a school project with her daughter. We edited it down to a three-picture combo. It was Lew's finest work. That night, as he walked down the hallway to the photo department, I yelled after him, "Hey, Lew, way to go ... thanks for the great pictures."

That was the last time I saw Lew Raines. He died in his sleep that night. He was 56. A bear of a man. A man who had talent.

You gotta believe.

Life is too short

After Lew Raines died, I thought, "My God, if ever there was a choice of what kind of manager I want to be – a motivating, supportive, nurturing boss, or a disciplinarian, butt-kicking boss – it was obvious that life (mine and others) is too short and precious for people to have to live with a rigid, in-your-face, military, my-way-or-the-highway management style.

Or to die with a chewing out as a final farewell.

6 THE MAGIC OF MOTIVATION

It starts with you

Your vision is to build the best photo staff possible and for that staff to generate a powerful photo report day in, day out. There are a thousand things you, as the leader/manager, can and must do to fulfill that vision, but the all-important key to success is MOTIVATION.

Motivation – that which emotionally moves a person, as in inspiration. Motivation – the trigger to action. Of course, people can be motivated in two ways – negatively through threat, or positively through encouragement. Motivation by threat, or in some cases by harassment, is inevitably self-defeating, at least when it comes to people in a creative field such as photography. Positive motivation, on the other hand, is about getting the best from people over the long haul.

As leader/manager, the magic wand of motivation is in your hands.

TOUCHING MOMENT Just hours before birth, Jeff Conlogue feels wife Stacey's contractions. Such an unpredictable image, pet dog included, only results when the photographer stays alert. Subtle moments often make for the strongest photographs. **Tamara** **Voninski**

Note: I consider the responsibility of the two job titles to be different. A person can be a good leader (inspiring) but a poor manager (not good at running systems), or, conversely, a poor leader but a good manager.

A good leader has a vision of great possibilities and motivates the staff to achieve that vision by setting high standards and inspiring the staff with lots of positive reinforcement, by making the workplace upbeat, rewarding and fun, by solving staff problems, fighting for better equipment and pay, by coaching and sometimes by just listening.

A good manager motivates the staff by organizing department systems to make sense, including scheduling (work shifts, photo assignments, vacations and training), digital photo production workflow and by making sure everyone is properly equipped and that equipment is well maintained.

All of these responsibilities, and many more, affect motivation and morale. In fact, everything you do as a leader and as a manager affects motivation and morale.

51 going on 19

Not long after I arrived at the Virginian-Pilot, one of the senior staff photographers, 51-year-old Robie Ray, told me, "You know, I haven't had so much fun shooting pictures in years. I feel like I'm 19 years old again." That's what positive motivation is all about.

Even if you are a military-style tough manager (who laughs at the idea of positive motivation), if you are a *smart* tough manager, you will practice positive motivation anyway because it is the smart thing to do.

Positive motivation is the energy that will drive your operation. It is the spirit that will inspire your staff to perform at its highest, most creative level; to perform with enthusiasm, passion and joy.

Motivation is everything. I can't over-emphasize that point.

As you would like

Throughout this book I will talk about the things I did that I feel helped motivate the staff, individually and overall. But possibly the most important thing I can tell you about motivating your staff is this: Treat everyone fairly. More specifically, treat everyone as you would want to be treated.

There were several ways we made things fair at the Pilot.

Everyone was treated the same when it came to equipment, work schedules and seminars.

That meant all photographers received the same camera equipment and equal access to a pool of the more exotic lenses and lights.

All 10 photographers in the downtown office rotated through all 10 month-long shifts – the good, weekends-off shifts right through to the "crappy" Wednesday/Thursday-off shift. When it came to desirable out-of-town photo trips, every photographer had their chance, with assignments based on the photographer's interest and ability. I kept a running account of trips taken.

The Politics of Housing

PLIGHT Dry stories, like federal budget cuts, need to be personalized. The Virginian-Pilot showed Georgia Williams, 76, cold, hungry and too weak to start her wood burning stove. After the picture ran, she got help. **Robie Ray**

Everyone was treated the same when it came to sending staffers – photographers and photo editors – to the annual state photojournalism convention. Taking turns was the policy. Same for out-of-state seminars and workshops, and in-house training (of course, needs were considered).

What about seniority?

You might ask, if photographers work for one newspaper for many years, shouldn't there be special rewards for faithful service? Like work schedules? Indeed, at many American newspapers veteran photographers have permanent Monday through Friday, daytime work schedules. Isn't that fair?

It might be fair from the photographers' point of view, but it is not fair to the newspaper's readers. This arrangement, in almost all cases I'm aware of, does not serve what should be the newspaper's No.1 visual mission: producing a great daily photo report. For the truth is, while some staff veterans are among the most talented photographers on some staffs, many of them are not. That means that these less-talented photographers are shooting many of the important news stories that occur during the day (when the majority of these stories take place), while younger, often extremely talented photographers are stuck on night shifts. This arrangement doesn't serve the visual mission. It's a bad idea.

At the Virginian-Pilot there were three exceptions to the policy of treating everyone the same. One was vacation time. The other two involved photo assignments and salary. Because the Virginian-Pilot is a non-union paper, we didn't have strict rules to follow.

When it came to vacations at the Pilot, seniority had its privilege, but with a limit. Those with seniority had their choice of vacation days. However, they had to pick their vacation days by the end of February. Once March arrived, all days that year not spoken for were up for grabs by anyone on staff.

Rewarding excellence

All photographers are not created equal. Some, because of natural talent or just plain old hard work (or both) consistently perform at the highest level, producing superior photographs daily. How do you encourage photographers to strive to perform at that level? By rewarding excellence. How? With carrots in the form of better assignments and better pay. Do outstanding work and you (the photographer or picture editor) will be recognized and rewarded.

Now, having said that about rewarding excellence, that doesn't mean your top performers get ALL of the good photo assignments. We're not talking a star system here. It means they get more of the choice assignments. But every photographer who is working hard and doing his or her best will get some of the good assignments.

If you do have a star system, in which one or two photographers are treated like royalty and the rest of the staff like serfs, you have a situation where a few people are happy as hell and a lot of people are mad as hell. Not the way to go. The overall staff will produce a much stronger photo report if everyone is relatively happy because they feel they are respected and being treated fairly.

Ironically, there was a reverse reality for the top-performing photographers at the Virginian-Pilot. They received more than their share of visually weak assignments – important news story assignments that called for photographers capable of pulling superior, storytelling pictures out of visual voids. In other words, they were constantly asked to come through in the clutch by making something out of nothing.

At the Pilot, better pay and more of the better photo assignments for those performing at a superior level was not a hidden agenda. On occasion I talked about it at staff meetings. No secrets. It was an open, straightforward message to encourage every staff member to strive to perform at his or her highest level. It was the carrot at work.

Doing the right thing

A good leader will care about and do what she or he can to support members of the staff with their personal family needs. The Virginian-Pilot was always generous about doing what it could. Photo department manager Bill ("Abby") Abourjilie and I once took more than full advantage of this company generosity.

Photographer Beth Bergman's mother was dying of cancer. Beth needed to go home to Massachusetts to be with her mother who lived alone. Abby and I said, "Go, and don't worry about the time." We didn't tell anyone in the newsroom. She continued on full pay. After three months we finally told the managing editor (the photo department being a long way from the newsroom helped a great deal in keeping our secret). Beth was then put on a partial-pay leave of absence. She was gone for another two months. Beth was with her mother when she died.

Some managers are forever worrying about setting precedents. "What if someone else … We can't afford this again … Now everyone will expect …" And so goes the thinking. All just negative, defensive thinking as far as I'm concerned.

Just do the right thing for God's sake. Let the future take care of itself. Things will work out.

Care about staff first

You care about the staff because it's the right thing to do. You'll feel good about it and, in return, the staff will be motivated to care about you and what it is you're trying to accomplish at the newspaper.

In the end, a staff that feels it is fairly treated will come together as a team, perform at its highest level and fulfill its photographic mission of excellence.

That's what happened at the Virginian-Pilot. Often, as I sat in my office and looked through the large glass windows into the photo department, I marveled at what I saw: A hothouse of creativity and sharing. Camaraderie. Staffers helping fellow staffers. Talking pictures. Editing images. Photographers. Picture editors. Everyone. And lots of laughter. Team. Excellence.

No, no, no

Okay, you've heard about some of the important "dos," now for some important "don'ts." While positive motivation is an ongoing energy-supply upper, there are things you can do the wrong way that can send a staffer into a tailspin.

Don't ever assume a staff person is guilty of a reported misdeed until you have spoken with the individual and then checked out all the facts. Oftentimes, what other people say about a person is based on rumor, or is just plain wrong. If you want to lose the trust and loyalty of a staff member on the spot, accuse him or her of something he or she is innocent of. Even if the individual has caused problems in the past, give that person the same respect and benefit of the doubt that you would give anyone else. Past performance is not proof of present guilt. In other words ... no vigilante hangings.

If you know someone is guilty of something – anything – don't ever reprimand them by note. Notes have no personality. Notes can't listen. Notes have no voice inflections. Notes are the ultimate cold, impersonal message. Oh, the anger they can generate. Always have the decency and respect to talk to that individual in person or, if you can't see them face-to-face, talk to them on the phone.

Don't be the too-busy leader/manager who has no time for staff members when they come to you for help. Don't give them, "I can schedule you in next Thursday at 2:30." Talk to them NOW. Or, if you are engaged with other people at that moment, just as soon as you can. Being open and available means NOW.

Remember, a ton of good will and good morale can slide downhill fast with just an ounce of insensitive managing on your part.

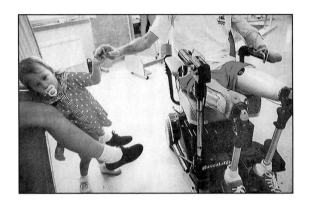

7 TAKING PHOTOGRAPHERS TO THE NEXT LEVEL

A pony under there somewhere

An amazing number of talented newspaper photographers produce good pictures for readers every day. But, many of these talented photographers also produce a lot of god-awful pictures.

Here's the problem at American newspapers: Photographer goes on assignment, sees a great picture situation, shoots a great picture. That's good. Photographer goes on assignment, sees a lousy picture situation, shoots a lousy picture. "Same ol', same ol'" and boring. That's bad.

There are, however, talented photographers in America who go on assignment, see lousy picture situations and shoot great pictures. Photographers call that "making something out of nothing." Most photographers come back with these pictures on occasion.

FAMILY The photographer tells a remarkably powerful story by not including William Kidwell's face and only his wife's legs. The father, legless and with only one hand as a result of a motorcycle accident, holds his daughter's hand in a poignant moment. **Bill Tiernan**

But the photographers who are performing at the highest possible level – those who are recognized as the best in the profession – come back from lousy visual assignments with compelling, special storytelling pictures virtually every time.

What separates these great photographers from the rest of the pack? Are they just plain better than the other talented photographers? Do they have a secret?

Well, first off, when they arrive at a scene that most photographers might describe as visual manure, these special photographers know that there is "a pony under there somewhere." We're talking vision here. A positive attitude. Pride. And sometimes just the patience to wait for the magic moment.

And perhaps most of all, beyond talent, I've observed over the years that the one thing that all the great photographers share is mental toughness. They are all bulldogs. They never give up on a shooting situation.

Former Virginian-Pilot photographer Michele McDonald wrote me, "You encouraged and expected the photographers who worked for you to take risks, to find a way to make our work sing, to make people want to take a second look. I learned to look again and again, and to notice what was easily overlooked in the familiar and commonplace. I learned to try to find dignity and meaning and beauty every day, in every situation I photographed. You, forever optimistic, looked for and found the best in us and made us want to live up to your opinion of us."

The real secret

And that's the good news for you – the leader/manager striving to lead your photo operation to the promised land of daily visual excellence. We're talking about something every photojournalist can do: take a challenging situation, and through a positive attitude and hard work, produce pictures that go beyond what conventional wisdom might expect.

Thus, we've answered the question "where do good pictures come from?" They come from all visual situations – good ones and bad ones. But the real secret is they come from the photographer's creative mind, individual effort and never-give-up attitude.

All newspaper photographers are not created equal. Some are, in fact, more talented then others; but *all* photographers have the ability to perform at a higher level – the next level.

And for those photographers not performing up to their true potential, the surest way to move to that next level is to start making something out of nothing (or finding a pony under all that manure) all the time. It can happen. They have to know that. You, the leader/manager, have to know that. It must become a part of the photo department culture.

I've seen photographers in Norfolk and throughout the country – once they get the idea – rise to a new, higher level.

The 1-point, 2-point challenge

Some years ago I began to see these Cinderella pictures in a new light. I saw the need to give photographers more credit for shooting outstanding something-from-nothing pictures than for shooting outstanding pictures from assignments loaded with great visual potential.

And so I created the "1-point, 2-point" concept to give special recognition to photographers who go to "bad" assignments and raise their photography to a surprisingly high level.

Thus, "good-from-good" photos became one-point pictures, and "good-from-bad" photos became 2-point pictures. From that idea came the "1-point, 2-point picture show" that I have been showing audiences ever since.

I originally figured it would be my talk for a year or two, but the response from photographers was so overwhelmingly positive that I have become the Johnny Appleseed of the 1-point, 2-point message. Photographers have told me that my slide show turned on a light bulb for them, that it was the first time they understood the real challenge of newspaper photography.

Pigs running everywhere

I start each show talking about an imaginary accident scene that has just occurred outside of the building where the talk is taking place. It might be that a gas tanker truck has been hit by a freight train and that truck and train are going up in flames. At the same time in all of the confusion, a truck carrying pigs skids on spilled oil and turns over. Pigs and people are running everywhere. And here come the firefighters and police. "Okay," I say, "all of us in this room – being the good photographers we are – will grab our cameras, run outside and start recording pictures." Then my question is: "How many of us are going to produce some outstanding pictures?"

The answer is obvious: All of us get good pictures. At a scene so described, the pictures practically take themselves. I call these 1-point pictures.

2-POINT CHALLENGE The story: how scary it is to go from junior high school to high school. Assignment: capture that feeling on the first day. Mission impossible? Not for this photographer, who clearly understood the power of body language. Lawrence Jackson

You've gotta be kidding me

During the slide show I describe a Virginian-Pilot photo assignment to illustrate a story about the trials and tribulations of students going from junior high school, where they are the top dogs, to high school, where they will be unknown nobodies. The assignment is to capture the apprehensive and nervous students making that scary leap on the opening day of high school.

"You gotta be kidding me," is what many photographers might say upon receiving such an assignment. It is certainly an easier scene to imagine than to actually find and photograph. But when I show the picture the Pilot ran with the story, two shy girls peeking around a doorway into the classroom they are about to enter, the 2-point "point" is made – a charming, compelling storytelling moment.

A dozen or so 2-point something-from-nothing pictures are included in the show, emphasizing the wonderful possibilities that exist out there in the world of bad assignments.

The 1-point, 2-point slide show starts with examples of my definition of 1-point pictures – the exhilaration of school graduations, the funny, sweet first day of kindergarten, happiness or dejection on election night, the in-your-face drama of breaking news. Situations in which any good photographer will make good pictures.

To emphasize that a 1-point picture is a 1-point picture no matter how many prizes it wins, I show the Pulitzer Prize-winning photo of the Oklahoma City fireman carrying a baby from the bombed-out federal building. A powerful, compelling picture. But the fact that it was shot by an amateur photographer (a banker) makes the point that any good professional photographer, given the opportunity, would also have recorded that dramatic scene.

Included in the 1-point category are not just pictures from visually rich photo situations, but also photo illustrations and environmental portraits. Since the photographer is in full control of these photos, there is little reason for them not to turn out successfully. And how about the sports action photos? Great pictures are the expectation. In most cases, the action is provided right there in front of the photographer's lens.

A bit of clarification here: Don't get the idea that 1-point pictures are not valuable. They are. Very much so. In fact every newspaper photographer's portfolio should include them – dramatic news pictures, photo illustrations, environmental portraits, sports action and any really good image from a good visual situation the photographer has been fortunate enough to record. But about half of the portfolio should be 2-point pictures – engaging surprises from those nasty "you gotta be kidding me" assignments.

A final point. The pictures to avoid like the plague are the zero-

1-POINT PICTURE Despite appearing on front pages around the world and winning a Pulitzer Prize, this dramatic image of a fireman carrying a baby following the bombing of the Oklahoma City federal building falls into Bob's 1-point category.

point pictures – cliché, predictable pictures still found in most American newspapers. Thoughtless "mug shots" of situations that look as if they were snapped by someone while sleepwalking.

Making 'The Board'

What is the best way to get across to the staff the message that coming back from "bad" assignments with "sleepwalking" pictures is not acceptable?

My solution – The Board.

Displaying staff photographers' work in the photo department or newsroom is not unusual. It's a great way to give photographers a pat on the back for good work. But the key is how you handle it and the standards you set.

At the Virginian-Pilot, The Board became incredibly important

THE BOARD Bob and Pilot staff photographer Huy Nguyen discuss the 2-point and 1-point staff pictures that Bob posted that week. The board pictures, a constant source of discussion in the photo department, set the Pilot's photographic standards.

in showing the way to do day in, day out superior work. Here is what I did:

- On an 8'x4' corkboard in the photo department, I posted staff pictures from the newspaper that I felt deserved recognition. Some were displayed on full pages, some I cut out. The selection was not done by committee. The choices were mine alone, which meant there was no confusion about what the standards were. If a photographer wondered why a picture did not make The Board, I was the guy to come to.
- I did not write comments with the pictures. I simply drew a red line under the credit lines.
- The first pictures to go up, of course, were the 2-pointers, but also any picture – including those from pretty good visual situations, if they had been ratcheted up a notch or two from the expected. The key to maintaining high standards was to be tough with what made The Board. "Pretty good" pictures, or pictures that didn't bring a little extra to the table, were out.
- While the standards were tough, it might be surprising that I did not use the same standard for all of the photographers. I considered each photographer's potential. If one of the less-skilled photographers shot a picture that was good considering his or her ability, the picture made The Board. But, if that same picture had been shot by a more gifted photographer, it might not make the cut. Of course, that could make things a little tricky. It wasn't something I talked about, but I think it was something everyone on staff knew at some level. Setting high photo content standards is critical, but it's also important to make sure each photographer is motivated by the display of his or her best work.
- I had three Virginian-Pilot newspapers delivered at home, one to pull tear sheets for The Board, one to check for press run quality control (more about that later) and one for the family. Each Monday, I took down the pictures from the previous week, through Friday. I then put up the good work from the Saturday, Sunday and Monday papers. By Friday of a typical week there would be 15 to 25 pictures on The Board.
- If I was running The Board today, I would also include outstanding staff photos published exclusively to the Web. I would post printouts of screen shots that show the picture and how it was displayed on the Web site.

In observing photo boards at other newspapers, I found that most were not effective. Too many of the pictures were not going to set high standards. They were "kinda good," "pretty good." Maybe they were posted simply because they weren't lousy.

The fact is, the daily photo report at many newspapers across the county can be described as content-deprived. An illustration of how bad-can-bad-be was driven home to the Pilot staff and myself after we subscribed for three months to a well-know newspaper. We chose this newspaper because that year it had won the National Press Photographers Association POY Best Use of Pictures award (primarily for its coverage of a hurricane). During our subscription, we were shocked to discover that the number of pictures that would have made the Pilot board numbered – are you ready for this – five! During the same three-month period, several hundred Pilot pictures made The Board.

While I'm sure this newspaper was deserving of recognition for its news coverage of a dramatic hurricane, it seemed obvious to me that on a daily basis its photographers had given up on any personal, creative vision. The pictures seemed to have been recorded by a staff that had been beaten down, and was shooting only what newsroom editors expected and demanded – familiar, safe, cliché pictures.

The heart of the matter

What was so interesting about The Board in Norfolk was that, over time, it became almost the living, breathing heart of the photo department. It became the focal point of lively discussions among photographers, photographers and picture editors, and even photographers and reporters. It also let editors, reporters and page designers who came into the photo department know that the staff was kicking butt. And it soon became obvious that photographers did not want to come back from their assignments with pictures that wouldn't make The Board.

The Board showed the standards, it was The Great Motivator. The Board was more than cork and tear sheets. I always felt that if it were ever taken down, the heart of the photo department would stop beating.

8 WHAT IS THE NEXT LEVEL?

Making the emotional connection

Now that we have established the merits of making something out of nothing, the question is: how do we do that?

First, not by trying to tell visual stories with images that merely present surface facts, that only duplicate or mirror words in the text of a story. The goal is to make images that supplement, reinforce and provide additional information, that create a different dimension that words cannot duplicate. To humanize the story, to create amazement, delight, laughter, sadness, concern and inspiration. We want to tell stories with images that make an emotional connection with the reader.

Says former Naples Daily News Managing Editor Bill Blanton: "Photojournalism has the potential to give readers an immediate, deeply felt insight into the news, an insight that goes far beyond

---

THE LONG WAIT How long does it take to capture that perfect, story-telling moment? For this image of Kay Abbotts shyly giving her final speech in the Dale Carnegie course in effective speaking, the photographer waited four hours. **Denis Finley**

the specific subject of the photograph. Its ability to communicate complex messages in simple images makes it a powerful – perhaps the most powerful – attractor of readers into our newspapers."

The most powerful of these images project real-life, candid human moments of universal truth and honesty. Moments – subtle or overt – that capture the essence of a personality, a situation or a mood. Moments that evoke a reaction, that put you there.

Do these pictures need to be further defined? What about body language, composition, lighting and stuff like that? What about over-using wide-angle lenses or telephoto lenses? Or shooting everything medium range. Sure, any of us could go into our definition of what constitutes success or non-success in these areas. But, as far as defining successful pictures, don't. As far as I am concerned, specific definitions only get in the way, like prison bars. Let your photographers fly free. Don't ask them to shoot to please you or anyone else. Shooting to please others is like painting by the numbers. No one has ever created a masterpiece by painting by the numbers.

And for goodness sake, don't you or any other editors or the photographers themselves, preconceive the pictures before the assignment is shot. Pictures in the mind's eye of people back at the office can never compete with the surprising, serendipitous possibilities at the assignment scene. Shooting what is preconceived is shooting the expected, the familiar, last year's picture, the cliché.

Let the pictures speak truthfully for the story. Understand that life is out there waiting. Let it happen.

Wild ride in the photo-mobile

Your advice to your photographers needs to be: Shoot for yourself, shoot from your gut. And for sure, take chances with your shooting, something that all great photographers have in common.

Once when I was giving my 1-point, 2-point slide show at the Northern Short Course, a young woman photographer asked me just how did one take chances shooting. After a moment of hesitation, I replied (as best as I can remember):

"On your next assignment, once you have finished shooting for the newspaper, pretend that you are taking an art photography class from a crazy teacher who wants you to shoot something totally wild and artsy-fartsy. So let your imagination go wild and make the kind of images the teacher can hang on her wall, but would never appear in a traditional newspaper.

"To get into the right shooting frame of mind ... imagine that you get into your photo-mobile (I use the projector control device to represent a car) and you head for this cliff. And as you get close to the edge, you give it the gas and over the cliff's edge you go (control device goes off edge of nearby table). That's where you want to shoot pictures for yourself and the imaginary art teacher. Down there in that wild, crazy canyon. Do anything you can imagine to come up with something different. The artsy-fartsier the better.

GOOFY GOLF Hey, don't be afraid to let photographers take chances, go a little crazy, see things differently, shake your readers out of their slumber, like this photographer did at the PGA Kingsmill Golf Tournament. Bill Tiernan

"Now pull your photo-mobile back up (I put the control device back on the table) and instead of shooting way back here where it is safe, as you always have, (the control device is now a foot or so away from the table's edge) you want to bring your photo-mobile right to the edge of the cliff (control device is now at table's edge). And that's where you want to shoot your real assignments – right there on the edge – where you tell the story with images that surprise, that are different, arresting and fresh."

Later I looked at the young woman's portfolio and sure enough, she was taking no chances with her shooting. And predictably her pictures were pretty ordinary. The following year at the Northern Short Course, she approached me with her portfolio. A very different portfolio, indeed. She said she had been driving that photo-mobile all year, taking chances. And her pictures showed it.

9 THE POWER OF PICTURE STORIES

Photojournalism's core

I'm happy to report that multi-pictures in story form – the venerable picture story page – is not dead. Its demise was gloomily predicted years ago when the cost of newsprint began to skyrocket. But this powerful form of communication is hanging tough at many American newspapers. As well it should.

Picture stories are at the core of what photojournalism is uniquely suited to do. Beyond what most single pictures can do, the combined force of multiple, coordinated pictures on a printed page (or in a multimedia audio slideshow) can take the reader to new levels of emotional involvement and understanding. Picture stories can shed light on the needs of individuals and the needs of society in ways word stories alone cannot.

POINT MADE Hampton Roads TV news anchor Terry Zahn gets the word about his cancer condition. By showing only the doctor's hand, Zahn's personal, lonely struggle against the killer disease is brought home to the viewer. **Martin Smith-Rodden**

At the Virginian-Pilot we considered it the responsibility of every photographer and picture editor to come up with picture story ideas. Alex Burrows (who would take my place when I retired from the Pilot) initiated the weekly picture story meeting. Each photographer was expected to always be working on his or her own picture story.

The meetings lasted only 15 or 20 minutes. We tried not to schedule photo assignments during the meetings, but they went on even if some photographers or picture editors could not attend. The main thing was to promote the message – picture stories are important. At the meetings each photographer reported on the story she or he was working on.

The picture editors worked hand-in-hand with the photographers to give them enough time to shoot and edit quality stories.

The stories are out there, that's for sure. Longtime National Geographic photographer Karen Kasmauski, who started her career at the Pilot, is one of the best in the profession at developing visual stories. She claims, "There are five stories on every block of every town and city in America." And just think, that's not even counting the countryside.

(Note: To learn about designing a picture page see appendix.)

PICTURE PAGE This page, and three photo-filled inside pages, told the story of a family's arrival in Norfolk, following their escape from Haiti. The layout demonstrates the power of a dominant image, played the right size, and the effectiveness of white space and a "soft edged" design approach. **Joseph John Kotlowski**

Respect Trust & Change

The newsroom challenge

⑩ A GOOD BEGINNING

The staff was pumped

"This photo department is no longer a service department."

With those words, a deafening cheer roared throughout the Virginian-Pilot photo department. It was my first day on the job. My first meeting with the entire staff.

I went on to say, "We are from this day forward a professional, independent department perfectly willing to work with any and all of the other professional, independent departments in this building."

It was a good beginning. The staff was pumped. They had anticipated this day with excitement, having heard what had been accomplished during the past three years at the Charleston Gazette in West Virginia.

ABOVE AND BEYOND It could have been just another boring assignment of a Marine command change at a podium. But not for a photographer dedicated to always coming back with images that are much better than what might be expected. **Michele McDonald**

Over the years, people have asked me how long it took to turn things around in Charleston and Norfolk. Only half joking, my answer has always been, "In about 15 minutes." When you bring the things to the job that I've talked about in this book so far, it really doesn't take long to turn things around.

Some Pilot editors and reporters signed on to the new teamwork way of doing things from the start. But some didn't. Right from the get-go, Pilot food editor Ann Hoffman resisted when we asked questions about her photo requests and suggested ideas for food illustrations. For Ann – a headstrong, but extremely bright and talented editor – it was still about the control game.

RED CHERRY Creativity was the order of the day when it came to food stories (about cherries in this case). The clown with a cherry "nose" spoke to the photo department's good relationship with food editor Ann Hoffman. **Bill Tiernan**

For three weeks she made it clear that our input was not welcomed. I'll never forget the day I walked up to her desk to discuss one of her food illustration requests, expecting her usual glowering look, but instead got a smile. It was over. Like that. She got it.

She realized we weren't the enemy. That we could all work together. From that day on she and photo collaborated beautifully, coming up with new, innovative and off-the-wall food illustration ideas week after week. She found us easy – and fun – to work with. Our goals were the same. Make the Pilot food section one of the best in the country. And together we did.

From that point on, Ann Hoffman became one of the photo department's best friends and strongest supporters.

One by one

And so it went. One by one the photo operation – with its new philosophy and professionalism – won over the other editorial departments. But for a time there was some natural resistance and resentment to the "new" photo department.

"Who do those people in photo think they are?"

Word editors and reporters had lost some of their traditional power over the one-time "service" department. Hey, we're talking turf here.

But as time went on, people in both newsrooms – the morning Virginian-Pilot on the fourth floor and the afternoon Ledger-Star on the third floor – began to realize the positive effect that the new photo operation was having on each newspaper. Much better pictures to go with stories. Picture editors who took much of the burden of dealing with photo matters off the backs of word editors and reporters. Soon, we were working together as equal professionals.

A TEAM EFFORT Bob (front and center) and the photo staff whoop it up after winning Best Use of Photographs for large newspapers in the annual University of Missouri/NPPA Pictures of the Year competition in Bob's second year at the Pilot.

As both papers improved visually and began to receive national recognition, I could feel the newsroom attitude about the photo operation shift from suspicion and resentment to appreciation and pride.

11 PICTURES ON THE PAGE

You can't just hope for the best

Shooting compelling pictures – pictures worthy of display – is one thing. Getting those pictures published in a way that best serves the readers is another thing.

Some photo managers take the position that it is not their job to influence what pictures are chosen for publication or how they are used. I disagree. You can't shoot 'em and then forget 'em. Or worse, just complain about their selection and use after the fact.

You can't just pass them to web or page designers and simply hope and pray. As leader of your photo operation, one of your all-important jobs is to see to it that the right pictures are selected and used effectively.

Getting the best pictures to the readers starts in the photo operation. The process is the same, whether the images will appear

---

HE CREATED ME Jim Ballou always knew he was different from other boys, but he got married at 16 nonetheless. Five years later they separated, and he said, "I accepted if God created me this way, there's a reason. He didn't create me evil. He created me gay." **Tamara Voninski**

in print or online. Here's the way it worked to get pictures onto the pages of the Virginian-Pilot.

Trust your staff

After the photographers had looked over their shooting takes, it was their job to pick out the very best pictures to tell the story. Photographers who wanted or needed help from picture editors to edit their shoot received it. I was also available.

Some page designers want to see lots of pictures in order to have lots of choices, even when they might only need one picture to go with a story. At the Pilot, the photo department didn't go along with that. We felt the photographer's job was to show their very best work. If one image was clearly superior to all other images, then they showed only that image. Editors don't ask reporters to turn in two or three versions of the same story. However, if a Pilot photographer or picture editor couldn't decide between, say three pictures, then they offered all three.

Further, if cropping would improve an image, Pilot photographers were expected to crop their own pictures to their maximum strength. In other words, to crop out what wasn't helping the picture, same as reporters are expected to edit out their own excessive words.

For those page designers and layout editors who want to see a picture's entire frame, the argument against this is that they don't ask to see words the reporters cut from their stories during the writing process. At the Pilot, if a given picture did not clearly connect with the story, then photographer, picture editor and page designer worked together to come up with a more successful image.

When the newspaper asks photographers to produce their very best work they should respect them enough to accept what they offer as their very best work. Treat them like professionals. Don't ask them for their best work plus "everything else you got."

At many newspapers where photographers do turn in their best pictures, plus their also-rans, the weaker pictures often end up in the paper. Photographers and picture editors must be trusted as experts of visual content if a photo operation is to succeed as a professional arm of the editorial process.

Teamwork, not territory

It's the page designer's job to take what's offered by writers and their copy editors, and photographers and their picture editors – their best work – and then design effective, compelling pages.

Does that mean designers have no say about stories and pictures that will appear on the pages they design? Of course not. They certainly have the right to say, "Hey, wait a minute, I think this story misses the point, or, I think this picture isn't true to the story." And designers particularly have that right, considering they are the architects of the pages. In a professional environment the goal must always be to produce the best pages possible.

When it comes right down to it, it's mutual respect and teamwork between the visual editor, the designer and the section editor that assures that the best pictures get to the reader, either in print or online.

On to the press

Also, at the Pilot, photographers did the first steps of preparing images for the press by doing their own dodging, burning and toning. The photographer's control of the final look of their pictures in the newspaper was considered to be part of their creative ownership. After the photographer finished preparing his or her pictures, Pilot imaging specialists (former engravers) then "put the numbers" on the images to achieve on the press the look the photographer was seeking.

Newspapers across the country that have taken the creative control of the image away from their photographers – oftentimes to keep them on the street shooting – are making a mistake if they truly care about giving their reader a quality product.

These final steps are just as important as any others in giving the strongest images to the reader. Think about an image beautifully dodged, burned and toned by a photographer to create just the right effect and mood, versus an image rendered uninspiring by a technician trying to guess what a photographer might have wanted; or worse, not really concerned what the photographer might have had in mind at all.

12 WORKING WITH DESIGNERS

An open affair

In today's most dynamic, best-designed publications the use of words, pictures and headlines is a sophisticated, creative blend that allows each to help guide readers effortlessly through the news. Pages are inviting and accessible. This was the case at the Virginian-Pilot. There was good reason for that and it started with picking the right pictures.

Traditionally, the selection of photos at most morning newspapers is made at the late-afternoon news meeting held in a meeting room. For those not invited, the decisions that emerge can seem wrapped in secrecy and mystery. "How and why did they come to that decision?"

THE FUNKY FACTOR Sharice Williams, 7, is teased by her twin brother Sean with a fish he caught at First Landing State Park. We don't have to see Sean or their father Scott to share this fun moment. **Stephen M. Katz**

At the Pilot, the afternoon news meeting was a completely open affair – held in the middle of the newsroom at the A1 designer's computer desk. Everyone had input; news editors, picture editors, the managing editor and the A1 designer. The local page designer was also invited. Photographers and reporters were welcomed. It was a wonderfully inclusive concept. And it worked.

The group decided where pictures and stories would go – in the A-section or in the local section. The A1 designer normally took the lead. Often she or he had the stories and pictures early enough to prepare several design concepts for consideration by meeting time. After the meeting the designers were left to consider everyone's input and then get on with designing their pages. (Note: each section front designer at the Pilot was responsible for one page per day.)

Self-evident

At the Pilot the designers were very good. The Pilot design philosophy was that good design was self-evident. It didn't need explaining. It was sophisticated. Designers didn't get cute with eye-catching design tricks just to show off. Well, occasionally they did. But for the most part they knew the design was not about them; that content was the star attraction. They knew their job was to present content (stories, headlines, pictures, captions, illustrations, graphics) on every page in the most compelling, pleasing and effective way – a way that the reader could logically and easily move through.

In effect, design is the reader's welcoming committee. Or another way to think about it – design is the picture frame for the words, photographs and art. But please, no gaudy picture frames – design elements that overpower content.

Good design speaks to a sense of organization (as artful as it might be) that engenders the reader's trust. Papers that are poorly designed give off vibes that say we're not organized, we don't really know what we're doing. And the next logical question for the reader is, "Can I trust what I'm reading and seeing in this newspaper?" So, in my mind, good design is important beyond being effective and artful.

NOT YOUR USUAL NEWS DAY When really big news happened, editors and designers at the Virginian-Pilot often devoted all or nearly all of the front page to the story, realizing that the story was all the readers would be talking about that day. So it was when the Navy's fleet sailed home to Norfolk, when the jury sentenced Oklahoma City federal building bomber Timothy McVeigh to death, and when terrorists flew airplanes into New York City's World Trade Center twin towers on Sept. 11, 2001.

Happily, the Pilot designers knew good storytelling pictures. They worked easily with the picture editors. They knew that, in order to make the emotional connection with readers, it wasn't enough for content details in a picture to simply be seen. They knew the picture had to run large enough to have impact – enough impact for the readers to feel the emotion the image had to offer.

A1 – A big hairy deal

The Pilot designers were particularly skilled and bold in designing page A1 for big breaking news, often taking the entire front page for the story (text, pictures and graphics). They weren't afraid to say to the readers – this is a big hairy deal. Stories that got this treatment included Hurricane Katrina, 9/11, the Oklahoma City bombing of the federal building and the Challenger space shuttle explosion. Hey, on those kinds of days, that's all your readers are going to be talking about. Newspapers that on really big news days still stick to what they do, day in, day out, are not in tune with their readers.

Style and substance

Each Pilot photographer had his or her own style of shooting. I encouraged them to shoot from their gut. Do it their way. Take chances. But always tell the story. That meant the Pilot designers dealt with a lot of pictures that didn't fit traditional molds.

To their credit, they were cool with these "different" pictures – pictures where people's heads are cut off at the shoulders (if that helped reinforce the storytelling impact of the image); pictures with blurred motion (when it fit the mood and theme of the story); body parts extending into the picture from odd angles (that added graphic intrigue). The readers certainly didn't go to sleep viewing our pictures.

In general, Pilot photographers had an open style of shooting, using a wide-angle lens to include not only the prime subject, but also the extended environment. And when it came to cropping, they often made their crops extreme – emphasizing either the horizontal or vertical strength of the visual flow of the image – that resulted in some interesting picture shapes.

For the designers, these open-style or extreme cropped pictures didn't seem to be a problem. The key reason was because they started the design of their pages by placing the lead picture on the page first. And then they built the page around the picture. By doing this, the designers were free to play the picture the size and shape it deserved to run.

At too many newspapers, designers box out a hole for the picture before they see it, and then go on to build the page. When the picture arrives they just crop it to fit the predetermined hole and squeeze it in. If the content of the picture deserves more space, well, it's too late.

The Pilot designers also understood that if a single picture accompanied a story, that picture did not have to always show the story's end result. They understood that a picture that shows a part of the story in progress – a visual paragraph if you will – also served the readers.

Two-picture combos were big at the Pilot. One picture ran as the dominant, impact picture. It was always the one that carried the emotional message of the story. The smaller picture's job was to set the scene. Very effective.

These practices, started when the "Norfolk Visual Revolution" was launched, became the cultural norm at the Pilot. The photo team worked hand-in-hand with the design team. We had our moments, but over the long haul we worked well together. Photo (the picture editors, photographers and myself) was always in on the planning. And the picture editors and I also did a lot of follow-up on how pictures were used in the paper the next morning. We offered suggestions – gentle suggestions. It was a learning process.

Expect the unexpected

Pilot readers came to expect their newspaper to show them pictures that were different, daring, surprising, creative, compelling, funky, emotional – but always storytelling. When I show some of these kinds of pictures to audiences of photojournalists, I am often told that "our newspaper would never run those pictures, our readers are too conservative." My answer to that is those who are really too conservative in their thinking are your editors in the newsrooms, not your readers. American readers have been brought up in a highly charged, visually sophisticated world. Think about some of the really good TV commercials, think about MTV, think about special interest magazines such as Time, Vogue, Rolling Stone, National Geographic and on and on.

Sure, all of us get some negative calls and letters from our readers about pictures. But believe me, our readers, no matter what part of the country they live in, are much more sophisticated than we give them credit for.

When we constantly feed them the same old cliché pictures their eyes must glaze over.

Now pinch-hitting

When I arrived, the Virginian-Pilot's design was uninspiring. Picture use was nothing to brag about either. Something needed to be done. With that in mind, I offered help to the business department, the weakest link in the paper's overall poor design.

I told the business department that we would be willing to design some of their pages. The business editors, with enough on their plates, welcomed the offer. I did some pages and I assigned one of the artists in the art department to do others (during most of my tenure at the Pilot, I oversaw the art department as well as the photo department).

One small step for the business section, one big design step in the right direction for the Pilot.

Some time later, it was apparent that the Pilot's features section – The Daily Break – could use some design help, too. At the time it was the artists who designed the pages. While the page presentation was adequate, it wasn't special. And there just happened to be someone I felt could do a better job. It was Roman Lyskowski, one of our picture editors.

I talked the two top features department editors, who were very open and progressive, into letting Roman take over the design of their pages, which included the Daily Break and the Food section. Roman did a terrific job, but left the paper a year later because of the Pilot's unfortunate nepotism policy.

At that point I talked another design-gifted staffer, photographer Rob Kinmonth, into taking over as the features department's designer. He was reluctant to give up photography, but finally agreed. Rob designed some wonderfully creative pages for four months, before asking to go back to his true love – photography.

The case for not listening

Inspired by what Roman and Rob had produced, the feature department editors began looking for a permanent page designer. With my help they hired Alan Jacobson. Alan, a talented photographer/designer from the Allentown Morning Call, soon impressed everyone with his innovative design skills.

The Pilot needed a major redesign, but the executive editor, who by this time was Sandy Rowe, was not ready for such a bold move. But because she was willing to take design baby steps, the features editors and I were able to talk her into letting Alan spend one day a week on "cleaning up" the Daily Break design. On the day he did redesign work, an artist designed that day's Daily Break page.

Sandy and others were pleased with the changes Alan was making, and she agreed to let Alan work two days on cleaning up the Daily Break, plus some of the paper's other pages. However, she warned that these design changes did not mean a general redesign of the newspaper was in order.

The features editors, Alan and I were not very good listeners at that point. Thus two redesign days turned into three, then four.

Finally, Sandy agreed that the Pilot needed redesigning and that Alan was the person to do the job. At that point Alan's full-time job was to completely redesign the paper. Five days a week. And a new features page designer was named.

The lesson is: Sometimes, for the good of the newspaper, not hearing the boss can be a good thing for everyone.

13 FIGHT SMART

Show respect

Convincing others in the newsroom to accept your way of seeing things – the selection of pictures, the size of pictures, the placement of pictures on the page – is always an interesting challenge. While there were many more successes than failures at the Gazette and the Pilot, I learned that some "victories" were not worth the cost. As time went on I learned when to pick my battles and that I didn't have to win every battle to win the war.

Probably the most important thing I learned in the newsroom was how to work with other editors. The key was to never make an argument personal. To never suggest that the person you were debating is not as qualified as you on the subject. To never say anything like, "But can't you see?"

I tried to always respect the other editors no matter how much

ON DUTY This documentary picture was part of a series about recent graduates of the Virginia Beach Police Academy. Officer James Webster talks with a mother whose son is accused of beating up the child being held by his mother. Ian Martin

we disagreed. I treated them as equal professionals. I always tried to recognize that their opinions were understandable considering their background and the practices and philosophies they had learned coming to that point in their careers.

The slightest attitude of superiority on my part would have meant death to that particular argument and probably to that relationship – a price I could not afford to pay. A price you, also, cannot afford to pay.

I always fought hard for my ideas, sometimes with great passion. Sometimes I joked with our picture editors that it was okay to occasionally jump up on a newsroom desk to passionately make your point. But really, I found the key was to be straightforward and respectful with everyone. That's what paid off. Great relationships were formed at the Pilot and a great photo operation became a reality.

DESKTOP DIPLOMACY Bob often expressed himself passionately in the newsroom. He joked with Pilot picture editors including Alex Burrows, left, that it was okay to jump up on a desk to express that passion. Staff photographer Vicki Cronis, while shooting Bob for an article, captured this image during a photo management meeting.

They notice

The readers noticed the successes too. One day a reader called me to compliment us on our photography. She said that she hadn't realized how "really special" the photography in the Pilot was until a recent trip out of town when she had the opportunity to look at newspapers from a number of other cities. Newspapers, she said, whose pictures were "lifeless" compared to the Pilot's pictures.

14 FACE-TO-FACE IN THE NEWSROOM

Patience and follow-up

I found that at the Charleston Gazette and the Virginian-Pilot some changes came quickly, but others came slowly. Patience was a virtue. Small steps, so long as they moved forward, were okay.

The idea that a compelling picture was worth four or five columns on the page and sometimes six columns, rather than the usual three columns, came rather quickly at both newspapers. But convincing some editors that a daring, more emotional image was a better choice than the obvious, literal recording – the kind of picture that they were used to running – was more of a challenge.

It took lots of patience. And lots of follow-up the next day, talking pictures and page design in general. Sometimes it was to

STAY LATE Tell photographers covering events to go early and stay late – a tactic that paid off when the Coast Guard honored Jeffrey Spruill, 20 (shown in framed picture), after he gave his life trying to save a drowning seaman. His mother holds flowers. **Paul Aiken**

compliment the page designer on how the picture use and the page turned out. Sometimes it was to gently suggest how the page might have been improved with a different approach to picture use.

In the end it means never giving up. Gently push, gently push. It was kinda like the ancient torture method of dripping water. One drop at a time until success.

Use their words

When there is a difference of opinion between you and a section editor or a page designer about what picture to use, I learned one thing not to do. Don't debate your points using typical photojournalist visual terms. Terms like: good composition, great lighting, beautiful color, aesthetically pleasing. And eyes will surely roll if you use the phrase "visual impact."

I found that word people were much more receptive if I used "their words." Words they would use to describe the strength of a reporter's text story. For example, I would say, "this picture ... (as in, this story):

- captures the essence of
- goes to the emotional core of
- captures the mood, the spirit
- puts you there
- takes you back in time
- shows the conflict between
- lets you feel the tension
- shows the reality
- shows the irony
- makes you laugh, cry, care, or want to help
- is uplifting
- is just plain funny

Well, you get the idea, as in, making the emotional connection with your readers.

Everyone has a stake

And if section editors come on as the "owner" of that section ... shame on them. So says J. Bruce Baumann, photojournalism icon and retired editor of the Evansville (Ind.) Press:

"At enlightened newspapers the features department does not belong to the features editor, the sports department does not belong to the sports editor. No section belongs to a particular editor. Ownership is universal. Everyone at the newspaper has a stake in making all of the sections the best possible."

In this context, I think the photo staff should be expected to exert its right to have a strong say in what pictures are used in the various sections and how they are used. Once again, teamwork is the answer.

When it comes to recommending the size a picture should run, remind editors and designers that surveys show that stories that run with pictures get more readership. The larger the picture the larger the readership.

And designers, please don't say you need a piece of "art" for your page when you are talking about the need for a photograph. Photojournalistic pictures are not "art." While some may be artful in nature, at their core they are visual news information with value equal to text.

15 BLACK AND WHITE VS. COLOR

To be or not to be

In today's world, color photography rules the roost. Most assignments are made with the presumption (or corporate mandate) that they will be displayed in color because that's supposedly what readers want and expect.

But what about those special pictures, and especially picture stories, that may be more effectively published in black and white?

This is typical of the kind of conflict a visual leader must learn to manage. News organizations have lots of rules and guidelines. A good manager must know when to contest a rule when it does not serve the readers' interest.

FACES IN THE CROWD   Look for faces in the crowd to tell a story, as this image does at a Navy ship's homecoming in Norfolk. The expressions on the faces of Michele Dill and Donna Holder tell it all as they search the ship's deck for their husbands. **Lois Bernstein**

At The Virginian-Pilot we felt that some picture stories, indeed, did work best in color. But we strongly felt that other stories – because of the subject matter – could best be shown in black and white, a medium that can eliminate distractions and create mood to make an emotional connection with readers. This is an important decision for the photographer to know from the beginning of the process, because directional lighting is more important for pictures displayed in black and white than for those that include color. (That's why old black and white movies that have been colorized don't look natural.)

At the Pilot, it was the photographer's choice whether to shoot their stories with color or black and white photo display in mind. We trusted and respected their professionalism. But even at the Pilot, the photographers knew that upper management was hot on color. So the deal was, if they shot a story in black and white they needed good reasons. It couldn't be "just because ..."

And shouldn't the vision and judgment of the photographer count? In telling their story shouldn't they be able to make the journalistic, artistic choice, to choose color or black and white, and not be restricted by arbitrary rules?

Pilot picture stories that we did in black and white included:

- An inside look at Virginia Beach homicide detectives solving a murder investigation. The two-part series included a picture of the gory barroom murder scene.
- A five-part series on a woman's battle with breast cancer.
- A story about a summer of drought in Virginia and how it affected the state's farmers.
- A photo essay on life and death in Haiti.
- A Labor Day picture spread of strong environmental portraits of workers at their jobs. Why black and white? It played to the blue-collar workers theme.
- A nine-month-long series following a high school senior class through the school year. Many situations were shot in low light where it is more difficult to hold shadow detail in color.
- An eight-part series on illegal guns in Virginia. One dramatic, gritty, six-column picture showed a young shooting victim on a gurney in a hospital emergency room. The picture was credited with helping persuade the state legislature to pass a tougher gun control law.

The great black and white hope

One powerful thing about black and white images is that the viewer's eye deals only with the basic elements in the image – lighting, composition and physical properties. In other words, the viewer doesn't have to deal with color, which can be garish and distract from the storytelling content of the photograph. But even if color itself is not a problem, black and white images can create a more emotional, somber mood when called for by the story.

Sometimes shooting a story in black and white simply gives the newspaper an opportunity to offer its readers a visual change. Color, color, color stories and then slip in a black and white story. You may have noticed that American advertisers do the very same thing. They sometimes make their ads black and white, rather than the usual color, in order to jolt readers' senses.

CRY FOR COLOR This clever image (looking for a different way to show people watching fireworks) was a refreshing success – in color. In black and white it has less impact. Nhat Meyer

Of course, color photography makes its own case for being a powerful storytelling medium. Color itself can be the key to making a photograph successful.

Many of the great photographs work because they are in color. Many because they are black and white. There are notable examples of both.

Great color photographs:

- The earthrise over the moon's horizon, shot from Apollo 8 by astronaut William Anders. Seeing the earth in its bluish grandeur is breathtaking.
- The shuttle Challenger exploding in a cloud of white smoke in

COLOR TELLS A STORY While this image of the explosion of the space shuttle Challenger, made by Michele McDonald, is powerful in black and white, as shown here, color added another dimension when it was originally published. Readers were able to see the telltale orange glow of the tragic explosion within the white smoke against the bright blue sky. Michele McDonald

blue skies over Cape Canaveral. Pilot staffer Michele McDonald photographed the tragedy for the Concord Monitor and the Pilot.

- The portrait of a young Afghan girl refugee with piercing green eyes photographed by Steve McCurry at a border camp in Pakistan for the cover of National Geographic.
- The Pulitzer Prize-winning photograph by Oded Balility of a Jewish woman defying Israeli security forces as they remove illegal settlers in the West Bank. It's an iconic picture of a lone citizen challenging the authority of the state. Muted colors of the scene give the photograph the look of a classic painting.

Famous black and white photographs:

- Robert Capa's blurred, grainy photograph of an American G.I. crawling through the water toward the beach at Normandy, made for Life magazine on D-Day, June 6, 1945.
- Dorothea Lange's portrait of a migrant mother huddled with her three children during the Great Depression, made for the Farm Security Administration.
- W. Eugene Smith's Life magazine photograph of a Japanese mother tenderly bathing her 17-year-old daughter, deformed from birth as a result of industrial mercury poisoning in Minamata.
- AP photographer "Nick" Huynh Cong Ut's picture of 9-year-old Phan Thi Kim Phuc, naked and burned from napalm bombing, running down Vietnam Highway One, screaming.
- Yousuf Karsh's portrait of Sir Winston Churchill, the bulldog English prime minister.

Famous black and white photographs that arguably would have been more effective if they had been shot in color:

- Associated Press photographer Murray Becker's picture of the the German dirigible Hindenburg, photographed as it burst into flames while attempting to dock at Lakehurst, N.J., in 1937.
- Associated Press photographer Joe Rosenthal's iconic picture of the raising of an American flag atop Mt. Suribachi on Iwo Jima.
- Life magazine photographer Carl Mydan's picture of General Douglas MacArthur wading ashore on the Philippine island of Luzon, making good his promise that he "will return" to the Philippines to defeat the Japanese.
- Boston Globe photographer Stanley Forman'a Pultizer Prize-winning picture of an anti-busing protester using an American flag and staff as a lance in an attempt to spear a pro-busing supporter at a rally in Boston in 1976.

The truth is, some picture situations could be effectively recorded in either color or black and white. Some work best in color and some best in black and white. The story and physical reality should determine the choice, not a corporate mandate.

16 FAKING OUT THE READERS

The nuclear option

Some tabloid publications survive on gossip, the fantastic and downright lies that titillate their audience. That audience is not our audience. Our readers demand real stories and news. Which means there is nothing more important in our profession than our credibility with our readers.

At the Virginian-Pilot there was a cardinal rule. Any photograph that a staff photographer recorded that looked like an honest candid photograph had better be an honest, candid photograph. Faking a shot was committing the "nuclear option." It was a fireable offense, just as making up characters or plagiarizing material for a story was for a staff writer.

Two staff reporters were fired for plagiarizing during my time at the Pilot. No photographers were fired for faking a supposedly

---

DRESS UP White was in fashion that year. This image to illustrate that fashion news to the reader is both imaginative and honest. No faking out the reader with posed "reality."
Bill Tiernan

candid picture. However, I must admit on several occasions I had my suspicions.

It's a sad truth in our profession that many of the enterprise feature pictures that grace the pages of some of America's newspapers and Web sites are, in fact, phonies. These are pictures that the photographers set up. They faked the "action."

Cruising for enterprise feature pictures is the staple, as well as the bane, of some newspapers' daily existence. It is an old problem. With the growth of newspaper Web sites, the need for a steady stream of new content every day has added even more pressure to produce enterprise pictures.

It's bad enough that some papers depend on these fluffy recordings, even if they are honest images, but the crime is that editors in many newsrooms and on the Web simply look the other way when photographers make a habit of staging the action.

I don't think they would do that if the authenticity of a text story or words being broadcast were in question. This double standard, in my opinion, speaks to the poor judgment and downright ignorance of some editors when it comes to their responsibility to present the truth to their readers in all cases. They seem to fail to realize that photographs are just as much content as words. Shame on the photographers. Shame on the editors. And shame on all of us for letting this scandal go on for so long.

When real won't do

We had what might be called a "reverse cardinal rule" at the Pilot when it came to photo illustrations. No photo illustration could look like a real-life situation. It could not look like a documentary photograph.

In other words, if we were doing a story on a string of recent bank robberies, we would never recreate a realistic movie-like scene of bank robbers running out of a bank with guns blazing. This dramatic, realistic-looking illustration could strike readers as a real picture (despite the small line of type below the picture reading "photo illustration" – a bit of information most viewers might never bother to read).

So if we were to do an illustration for a general story about bank robberies, the rule was to make it, through exaggeration or by other means, clearly recognizable as a made-up picture. Effective, but fake.

All of this is in the interest of protecting the integrity and credibility of news documentary pictures. To do otherwise leads the reader to question all news documentary pictures that appear in the newspaper, and thus to question the very integrity of our publication.

There are, of course, legitimate posed "people" pictures. Like the fashion picture, as long as the models' poses are exaggerated and clearly not candid. Or the environmental portrait. If a picture shows a store owner standing proudly in front of his store, no reader is going to think it is a candid picture that the photographer just happened to shoot as he or she walked past.

NO FOOLING Environmental portraits are honest. This posed, Labor Day environmental portrait (of James Night, a slaughterhouse worker) is easily understood and doesn't create false impressions. **Denis Finley**

A matter of survival

But the bottom line is, all of us in the photojournalism profession must use our good, common sense when it comes to presenting content in our photographs, as well as in our text stories, and to hold ourselves to the highest possible standards when it comes to protecting our credibility with our readers. The survival of our profession depends on it.

17 TYPE IN NEWS PICTURES

Out damned spot

As good as the Virginian-Pilot's design was, something that drove me crazy during one editor's reign was his approval of type on next-day news pictures.

Unfortunately, it's something many American page designers don't seem to have a problem with. Documentary news pictures are the core of our mission to visually inform readers. When readers pick up the newspaper the next day, these news pictures must clearly say "here is the way it was." Our credibility is on the line.

If we treat these next-day news pictures merely as partial design elements, then I think the message for the readers is a bad one. By placing type in these pictures, the content is compromised (other words I can think of are diminished, weakened, interfered with, polluted).

ALL TOGETHER Body language, converging lines and an incredibly colorful evening sky (trust me) come together to create a well composed, powerful image of the Tidewater Tides opening day baseball game in Norfolk. This is a good example of a photo that would be ruined if type was placed over the dramatic sky. **Nhat Meyer**

Some people argue that everyone at a newspaper gets edited. That's true. Certainly reporters get edited to improve the content of their stories. For photographers, cropping to make the visual content stronger is editing. But putting type in pictures is not editing; it's a design technique. It is placing a non-visual, foreign element into the content of the visual story. It would be like slipping gibberish into the flow of the text of a reporter's story.

I'm being hard-nosed here only with documentary next-day news pictures. I feel that some pictures in a newspaper setting can work with type, if done with sophistication: Pictures that don't depend on news credibility. Pictures such as photo illustrations and feature page pictures. Also, old news pictures used to illustrate advance and retrospective stories are acceptable candidates in that their news credibility is not the issue of the day.

And it's important that if there are plans to use type on a staff picture for a feature page, then the photographer must be in on the planning from the beginning, before shooting starts.

Eyewitness reality

But we're talking NEXT-DAY documentary news pictures here. This is an argument about presenting them to the readers without distractions – about not getting arty with them and not having them associated with soft feature pictures. This is about presenting news photos as hard-edged, eyewitness reality – straight and simple.

One might argue that a next-day news picture with type within its frame – for instance a representational regional weather picture – might actually connect with a reader's visceral senses. And for the sake of argument, say it is true some of the time. But even if that's the case, is doing it some of the time worth it in the long run, considering the possibility of undermining the credibility of next-day news pictures in general, thus undermining the credibility of the newspaper overall?

Although I encourage page designers to be creative, when creativity compromises a higher concern – in this case credibility – it is creativity gone bad. Credibility must always win out.

Thus, when it comes to type in next-day news pictures the policy needs to be clear – just don't do it.

The effect on the morale of photographers whose next-day news pictures have been "typed" is no small matter. I can recall when one Pilot photographer received a note from an editor complimenting him on his A1 news picture that morning, a picture half covered with type. He sent the well-intentioned note on to me with a one-word comment: "Sigh."

One editor was happy with the picture. One photographer's morale was going down like a slowly leaking flat tire.

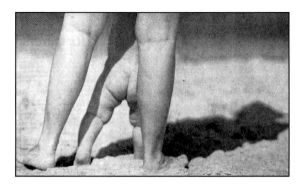

18 POLICY OR MYTH?

No bodies?

The day I walked into the Gazette as the paper's first-ever graphics editor, one of the other editors looked up at me, head tilted knowingly to the side, and said, "Something you should know. The way to survive around here is to always cover your ass."

For the most part, that meant not doing certain things that would upset Ned Chilton, the legendary, liberal, feisty Gazette publisher, famous for walking through the newsroom sockless – and sometimes without shoes – bellowing edicts as he went.

One of Chilton's edicts, so it was said in the newsroom, was that the Gazette never ran pictures of bodies. The day that a wire picture of murdered Italian Prime Minister Aldo Moro came in I was warned, "You can't run that picture. Ned won't allow it. We never run pictures of bodies."

I said, "Never?"

The picture, taken from what was probably a third or fourth

HOT WEATHER There are probably not too many newspapers in America that would run this picture. But hey, lighten up. It was really hot that day and little Lucas Jelinek, with his mom Nicky, is only 2 years old. **Beth Bergman Nakamura**

floor window in a nearby building, showed the prime minister's body curled up in the open trunk of an automobile parked on the street below.

I thought to myself: This is big news. Why in the heck shouldn't we show our readers this picture?

I walked into Chilton's office with the picture and told him that the Italian prime minister had been murdered. I asked, "Do you see anything wrong with running this picture?" Chilton answered, "No. Looks like a good picture to me."

"Well, the reason I asked is because they told me out in the newsroom that you had a policy against running photos of bodies."

Chilton answered, "What policy?"

Check out those newsroom policies, they may just be newsroom myths.

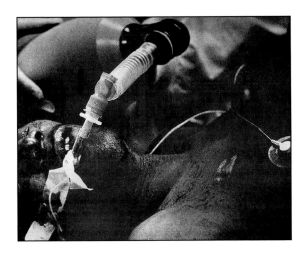

19 THE CASE FOR PICTURE EDITORS

A need indeed

Some newspapers today still don't see the need for picture editors in the newsroom, or at least for picture editors with real authority and influence. So it was at the Gazette. Except for Editor Don Marsh and a few others, the newsroom didn't have a clue about how much they needed a picture editor.

But the newsroom – and I, for that matter – were in for a surprise even before I officially took the graphics editor position. I spent two weeks at the Gazette trying out for the job. During those two weeks it was like a circus. A wonderful, fun circus. Everyone came to me to help solve their photo needs. When they started

GRIM REALITY This picture of gunshot victim Tony Hawkins of Norfolk, published in an 8-day series on guns in Virginia, helped lead to gun law changes in the state. Hawkins died later that night. We made a personal visit to Hawkins' family to get approval to run this picture. **Bill Tiernan**

lining up, I thought I might have to give out numbers – like in a butcher shop. It was great. I knew they needed help and I knew I wanted the job.

A full-time job

At the Gazette, I started out with four photographers. As graphics editor I coached the photographers, made the photo assignments (making sense out of them first), edited film, selected Associated Press wire pictures, made the call on wire and staff picture use, designed all of the full-page picture pages and picture combos, worked closely with the production crews on picture page layouts and with the press room on picture reproduction and color registration, and much more. Take my word for it – it was a full-time job. Twelve-hour days, and longer, were not unusual.

Through my experience in Charleston and from what I observed from watching the picture editors under me at the Virginian-Pilot do their jobs, it became clear that a picture editor has not only a critical job, but probably the toughest job in the newsroom. He or she, unlike any other person in the newsroom, works with every other editorial and production department in the building, almost on a daily basis.

Wisdom of Solomon

This person must be a leader, have good news judgment, and possess the wisdom of Solomon, serving both the interests of editors and reporters and photographers, people who don't always see things eye-to-eye. The challenge for any picture editor is to stand evenly with one

WHICH WAY DID HE GO? Picture editors need to look for body language. Here it adds interest and a little humor to this picture of two Virginia Beach police officers trying to figure out the escape route of a gunman who robbed a local bank.
David Hollingsworth

foot in the word camp and one foot in the photographic camp.

For some picture editors who once served as staff photographers, it is hard not to favor the viewpoint of photographer friends and peers when it comes to picture selection and use. On the other hand, I've seen picture editors, whether they had been staff photographers or not, favoring the viewpoints of the newsroom news editors – because the editors they worked with elbow-to-elbow every day had become their new friends and peers.

But the gold standard of picture editing is the picture editor who, despite pressures from either side, first and always serves the interests of the most important people – the readers.

Three to one

Many small newspapers don't have picture editors, because they either don't see the need or feel they don't have the money for such a position. Believe me, every newspaper needs at least one picture editor (without one – inefficiency and chaos; with one – coordination and a better photo report). Interestingly, there is an in-house solution in which money need not be a major factor.

If a newspaper has four photographers, convince one of them to become a picture editor. The one serving as picture editor – planning and coordinating assignments, helping to edit images, just being in the newsroom to know what's going on, plus helping others with all things photographic – that person will be worth her or his weight in gold. The bottom line is the paper will get at least as many pictures (and better pictures) out of the three photographers as they were getting out of four.

What happens if no one wants to be the picture editor?

Don't make the mistake of asking a photographer to be half photographer/half picture editor. That's a lame solution. As with other editing jobs in the newsroom, it's not a part-time job.

Rotating the four photographers through the position for three months at a time might seem like it would be a good solution, but temporary editors are less effective because they lack authority and aren't able to take advantage of relationships built over time.

The best strategy is to sell your best candidate on taking the job for at least, say, three months. That's enough time for you and the new picture editor to see whether he or she enjoys being a picture editor and is making a difference on the job. Offer lots of positive reinforcement when the new picture editor is doing a good job. It's important for both the new picture editor and the rest of the newsroom to recognize how this new position is improving photography and display.

But, if the photographer-turned-picture-editor is truly unhappy, or is not making a difference, then let him or her return to their photography position. If you're lucky one of the other two photographers will be a viable candidate.

One last thought. I think it is highly likely that even going from a staff of three photographers to a staff of two photographers and one picture editor can work. It would be worth a try.

20 MAKING SENSE OF PHOTO REQUESTS

Turning priorities upside down

The first big change I made after coming aboard at the Virginian-Pilot was to turn the photo assignment priorities upside down.

As with many newspapers, photo requests poured in like water from a broken spigot. They arrived from every editorial department – news, features, sports and business. Lots of routine daily assignments. And it was these easier, less time consuming assignments that went to the head of the line. A typical conversation at the photo desk might sound like this:

"Sorry, we can't do that drought-stricken farm family. That'd take at least three days. We're swamped with assignments. And

REAL LIFE Documentary photojournalism like this really drives home the effect a drought can have on a farm family. For farmers Mary Jean and John Evars it was constant stress and worry with budgeting down to the pennies. **Denis Finley**

that food illustration the food editor wants to do at the beach. No way. Can't we just shoot the food in the studio?"

The merit of the stories or their visual potential didn't count for much. Editors and reporters simply continued making routine assignments until there were no photographers left. The routine assignments were eating the really good assignments for lunch.

The service department mentality was alive, but not for long. I soon turned the photo assignment philosophy on its head. First to be assigned would be that out-of-town drought story. And the food illustration would definitely be shot on location at the beach.

Take two and I'll see you in the morning on Page One

After committing to the assignments with the most merit, we then got to as many of the other assignment requests as possible.

The new assignment philosophy was this: time equals quality images. That meant that each photographer, instead of averaging four to five assignments a day, would average two assignments a day.

Out went the grip-and-grin assignment requests – the check passings, the plaque holdings, the shovel-wielding dignitaries at groundbreakings and other assignments of dubious visual merit. Many of these kinds of assignments were completely killed.

After I arrived at the Pilot we changed the title "photo assignments" to "photo requests." A photo request wasn't a photo assignment until it had been approved by a photo editor. Language is important.

If you cruise you lose

One of the problems at the Pilot in the early days was that far too many stories that appeared in the newspaper were process stories. That is, stories about government and business activities, such as meetings and announcements, not the kinds of stories that produce meaningful pictures. Thus, we were forced to ask photographers to do a lot of enterprise cruising for feature pictures.

Thankfully, upper management finally figured out that a system that relied mostly on process stories was a system that was not serving the readers well. It was boring them to death. A major reporting shift was initiated that put much more emphasis on people stories and how the news affects people. The quality of the photo assignments improved immensely. For the photographers, the need for cruising for enterprise pictures became a rarity.

Newspapers today that still depend on their photographers to cruise for enterprise pictures to supply most of their daily needs – for whatever reason – are working with a broken system. They need to get a plan. One that matches photo requests with stories. People stories always help.

Whose job is it anyway?

One of the worst practices we had to break the reporters and editors of was filling out photo requests describing the exact picture, or pictures, they expected the photographers to shoot. The photographers called these requests "f/8 and be there." No thinking required.

Of course, our reply was: "Thank you very much, but just tell us what the story is about, and the photographer – at the scene – will figure out the best way to tell the story visually. Trust us."

Our message was: "Don't tell us what to shoot. However, ideas and suggestions are okay." I encouraged the photographers to welcome them. "If a dog walks up and gives you a good idea, be grateful. Then make sure you take a picture of the talking dog for the newspaper." The bottom line is, good pictures are what it's all about. It doesn't matter who originated the ideas.

So our goal was to improve the assignments by finding out as much about the stories as possible. We talked to the reporter, read a copy of the story or called the subject. While we had the authority to kill photo requests, we rarely did so. That was not going to win friends. But if improving them proved impossible, a picture editor talked gently to the assigning editor or reporter – and then the misguided photo request was dispatched to the bone yard of bad assignments. As time went on, fewer and fewer such requests appeared at the photo department door.

If the "bad" request – such as people grinning for the camera at a check passing – was to illustrate a story that actually promoted a good cause, whenever possible we instead tried to arrange an assignment that would show how the money was to be used.

When it came to ground breakings, we covered them if they were of public significance. However, forget the shovels. The photographers were to look for natural, candid moments involving the groundbreaking. It could be children of the dignitaries playing in the dirt behind the grownups. In other words, ditch the 10 grinning shovels and offer the readers an interesting picture that showed that the event had taken place.

Shooting blanks

Also, out went the assignment requests that produced pictures that rarely got into the newspaper. Many newspapers across the country have very poor records when it comes to the number of pictures shot vs. pictures published. I know of one metropolitan paper in the northeast where pictures from only 40 percent of the assignments were published. Now, that's just crazy. Talk about wasted resources – human and otherwise.

At the Pilot our publication record was 90 to 95 percent. While our photographers were asked to produce fewer pictures per day, pictures from almost every assignment they shot got into the newspaper. Imagine the morale of a photo staff that worked all day to get only half of its pictures into the pages of the newspapers. How many reporters would be happy if every other story they wrote never saw print?

My advice is – keep your shooting schedule average to two assignments a day for each photographer. Three is okay sometimes. And there will be days, if a couple of simple assignments are located close to each other, it could be more. But that will be balanced out when a photographer needs all day or more to do one assignment justice.

In giving photographers time on assignments to produce quality work, newspaper management and design consultant Bill Ostendorf says it gives them the opportunity to "go early and stay late." Ostendorf points out (preaches, really) that often the most intriguing, storytelling visual situations take place before the official event gets underway, or after the event has officially concluded.

Less is best

The two-photo-assignments-a-day scheduling is practiced by every newspaper I know of that is giving their readers a superior daily photo report. By lightening the shooting load, they fill their pages with consistently good images.

Newspaper photo departments that run their photographers all over the landscape day in, day out like panting dogs, shooting four, five and six assignments a day, are just kidding themselves if they really care about producing pictures that the majority of their readers care about.

21 PLANNING YOUR WAY TO SUCCESS

Can't start too early

When it comes to producing a great daily photo report, thinking ahead on important stories is critical. We're talking about identifying these stories early on. Brainstorming. Planning. Figuring out how to best cover them photographically long before they get into the hands of the photographer.

The old saying in the newsroom, "the first one with a plan wins," should be the guiding principle for the photo department. Take the initiative, use good judgment, and the photo department can take control of its own destiny when it comes to photo assignments and producing meaningful, storytelling pictures.

The photo department can never start planning photo coverage

ACCESS Independent voter Alice Folder had access to Sen. John Warner, as did the photographer. Access like this comes from early planning and the photographer developing contacts. **Beth Bergman Nakamura**

of stories too early – from complex, in-depth stories to even the simplest daily assignments.

At many newspapers this is not the way it works, of course. At these papers it's routine for photo requests to show up at the photo desk the day before the story is to run – a story that perhaps has been days in the writing. There can be several reasons for this failure. One is plain old bad habit. Another is reporters who don't like to talk about stories they're working on because word editors have a habit of grabbing their stories for publication – "we have a hole to fill" – before the reporters consider them finished. But successful planning includes picture editors early on ferreting out all stories and their picture potential.

The universal planning meeting

A key part of your job as leader of the photo operation is to convince editors in the newsroom of the merits of having a picture editor, and possibly a photographer, in on the first planning meeting of every significant story.

Story planning meetings at the Pilot were a way of life, held sometimes in the newsroom, sometimes in the photo department. Everyone there – photographers, reporters, picture editors and word editors – brainstorming strategy (word and pictures) for coverage of upcoming stories. This was done for major news events, in-depth socially significant stories and big sports events. No one person owned these stories. Everyone was free to offer ideas. It worked, which, in turn, meant the readers were offered superior results in text and pictures.

Teamwork

At the Pilot, two newsroom advance picture editors were responsible for working with the paper's many different reporting teams. Teams such as education, city hall, military, business, federal, state and sports. Each team's photo requests came through their "personal" advance picture editor. Photo requests and picture flow were smooth, and when problems did pop up, everyone knew who to go to.

The team that benefited as much as any department was sports. As with many sports departments, the sports reporters and editors – when it came to thinking about photo coverage – pretty much only kept their eye on the next games coming up. But sports team picture editor Bill Kelley was always thinking ahead, making sure the coverage for big games and events was initiated far in advance.

In the mix

The physical location of picture editors in the newsroom is critical to the visual mission. Make sure you have a photo desk in the middle of the newsroom, preferably next to the news desk. Now you have picture editors talking directly with news editors and reporters. Communication, communication, communication.

How many picture editors does a newspaper need? It depends on the size of the newspaper and its editorial staff. Some very large newspapers have a dozen or so picture editors. Some of these picture editors serve only individual departments, such as sports or features, or only handle projects.

But, at the minimum, every daily newspaper should have all seven days covered, one way or the other. Mornings are important for planning, getting photo coverage underway, and keeping the photo report up to date on the Web. Nights are important for editing late photo assignments for next-day stories, for seeing to it that the photo plans of the day are carried through to the press and for planning early-morning photo coverage that will cycle online.

The photo desk photographer

For many years at the Virginian-Pilot we had a photographer assigned daily to the photo desk. This photo desk photographer was only assigned daily news stories. She or he had the choice of that day's best news assignment. But if there was no such assignment that day, the photographer looked for community events to cover. If a real news event broke, the photo desk photographer covered it.

We went to the photo desk photographer system to avoid the problem of having all of our photographers committed for the day to shoot assignments for other departments, leaving the news desk without photo coverage options for an unexpected local story that could visually support the news pages.

Missing in action

In any circulation area there are many good – sometimes great – stories that go unreported. While it is all but impossible to know about and cover every deserving story, that doesn't mean newspapers can't do better. And while the responsibility of digging out these stories falls on everyone in the newsroom, it falls particularly on staff photographers. I say this because photographers are the newsroom's eyes and ears out in the community. They're here, there and everywhere covering photo assignments. Seeing things. Talking with people. As journalists they should always be looking for these obscure stories, regardless of the photographic potential. Then they need to speak up and share these story ideas back in the newsroom.

Also, in many newsrooms, good picture opportunities are being missed when reporters and word editors fail to recognize the visual potential of stories they are working on. Thus, no photo request is turned in to the photo desk. Some stories, indeed, may appear to offer little visually, but an alert picture editor can sometimes "see" the picture possibilities.

Two approaches can help avoid these missed opportunities. First, picture editors need to build a positive relationship with everyone in the newsroom to encourage open discussion about picture possibilities on every important story. Second, picture editors must know what stories are being written in the newsroom so they can suggest picture possibilities, instead of waiting for a photo request that might never arrive.

Visual opportunities are also missed when photo requests do come in, but the reporter has picked the wrong storytelling situation, the wrong place, or the wrong time of day – or all three. Some reporters arrange for an assignment to be shot at a time that won't disturb a subject's busy schedule. That may be too much consideration for the subject and not enough for the photographer whose best chance to record meaningful, documentary pictures is when the subject is busy. For example, some editors and reporters will schedule a request outdoors at high noon on a sunny day, when the subject is free, but the sun creates the harshest shadows – a photographer's nightmare. That's why picture editors must carefully monitor all photo requests that come across the photo assignment desk. At most newspapers too many are simply rubber-stamped.

PICTURE EDITING AT THE VIRGINIAN-PILOT, A CASE STUDY

During my time in Norfolk, the Virginian-Pilot was a morning paper with a circulation of 190,000 daily and 230,000 Sunday. There were as many as 18 staff photographers and four full-time picture editors – two daytime newsroom advance picture editors, a night newsroom picture editor and a photo department manager/assignment editor. With the help of photographers filling in as part-time picture editors, five weekdays and all seven nights were covered.

The two advance picture editors worked 9 to 6, Monday through Friday. One worked with the news teams and the other with sports, feature and business teams. The night picture editor worked from 2 to 11, Tuesday through Saturday. Staff photographers filled in on Sunday and Monday nights. The photo department manager/assignment editor worked out of the photo department Monday through Friday, 8 to 5. He was also responsible for equipment, supplies and keeping track of the budget.

As the assistant managing editor for graphics I attended planning meetings and occasionally filled in as a picture editor. Photographers would often bring pictures to me when they wanted my help with an edit.

PICTURE EDITING AT THE CHARLESTON GAZETTE, A CASE STUDY

The Charleston Gazette is a morning paper. When I was there it had 58,000 daily circulation and 75,000 on Sunday. We had a staff of five photographers. I was the graphics editor, which meant I was the picture editor and a designer. I oversaw all photo assignments and pictures that went into the paper (staff, wire and others) and did all of the full-page picture layouts and picture combo layouts. The chief photographer made photo assignments. He worked Monday through Friday, 8 to 5. He was also responsible for equipment, supplies and keeping track of the budget.

At the Pilot we sometimes asked editors and reporters to turn in some photo requests without setting the place and time, in order to allow a picture editor or the assigned photographer to call the subject and arrange for the best story-telling location and time of day to shoot.

Volunteer for action

When it comes to covering the news, normally it is the news department that sets the agenda. Sometimes at the Pilot, photo set its own agenda. The paper covered a lot of big stories in Washington, D.C., about 200-miles north of Norfolk. Occasionally, when Pilot news editors decided not to cover a D.C. event that we felt was a big story and had an excellent opportunity to provide our readers with meaningful news pictures, we sent a photographer anyway.

the Art of Hiring

Building a great team

A NOTE ABOUT HIRING

My thoughts on hiring photographers and picture editors take up a considerable part of this book. Not nearly enough time and energy is invested in this area at many newspapers. In the next 13 chapters I'll tell you several stories about hiring and encouraging some very special people during my career. Stories that will speak to such things as looking for a role model, thinking beyond convention to bring the right person on board, and looking nationally, no matter the size of your newspaper. Some of the things I'll discuss in these chapters also include:

- The importance of hiring and who to look for.
- Where to look and what to look for in a photographer and a picture editor, plus a few hiring don'ts.
- The importance of hiring minorities.
- What to look for in portfolios (plus tips for job candidates).
- Conducting a successful interview.
- How to make the job offer irresistible (and how to treat those who didn't get the job).
- Hiring interns.
- Dreams come true for young photographers, and older photographers too.
- Tips for photographers and picture editors looking for jobs.

22 HIRING – IT'S *YOUR* JOB

Not something you can hand off

Now we come to the most important responsibility of a leader/manager – HIRING. Over the years I learned that it doesn't get any more important than that.

Hiring is so important that you, as the leader/manager, must take full charge of hiring the right people. It is not something you can hand off to subordinates. It's your job. It is your responsibility. You cannot let other duties interfere, because every photographer and picture editor you hire must be that very special person who every day will make a positive impact on your newspaper's photo report.

When a staff position comes open, you must personally exhaust every effort to hire that right person.

BEHIND THE SCENES Two Norfolk police cadets, Donna Ripley and Carol Sargent, make sure they graduate in style, while Sargent's husband, Ed, looks on. This image proves that it can pay off big time to go backstage to avoid the typical cliché ceremonial picture. **Karen Kasmauski**

Remember, to achieve the Great Photo Report, it will take:

- The VISION that the staff can and will produce a great photo report.
- The sky-is-no-limit photographic STANDARD
- POSITIVE MOTIVATION to inspire every photographer and picture editor on staff to perform at her and his highest possible level
- And HIRING THE BEST possible people.

You cannot afford to make a bad hire.

No singles hitters, please

But what happens if you do make a bad hire? Think of it this way – using baseball lingo – you either want to "strike out" or you want to hit a "home run" with your hire.

If you hire someone who almost immediately proves to be a mistake – a "strike out" – you have the option of letting them go. The worst thing that can happen is to hire someone who is only so-so (a "singles hitter") who is not bad enough to justify removal. The problem is, when the new hire turns out to be a weak "hitter" more often than not they leave the photo operation stranded on base. Photographer or picture editor, they will stick to your newspaper like a fly to flypaper. You're stuck with them, possibly forever. And if they do try to get a job elsewhere, you

---

HIRING PHILOSOPHY: THINK CHARACTER

Every newspaper photo manager has his or her own philosophy when it comes to hiring. During my 20 years as a leader/manager I hired 31 full-time photojournalists, plus nine artists.

My basic hiring philosophy was to seek the most talented people who might be interested in coming to our newspaper. Beyond that, I looked for people of special character and depth, people who were journalists in the sense that they cared about the newspaper's mission of public responsibility, as well as being passionate about journalism. I wanted high-energy people. Self-starters. Team players. Ethical and honest. People with varied experiences and backgrounds. They read. Were good listeners. People of good heart, who cared about others.

might not be lucky enough that they get that job. "Singles hitters" may be nice people – but year after year they just trip along doing routine work. Will they make an impact on your newspaper? No. That's a price too high to pay.

When it came to hiring photographers, the worst advice I ever got was from a director of photography at a well-known newspaper in the South. He told me that he never hired the best photographers because they might cause staff dissension and unhappiness. Through jealousy, I suppose. So it seems this photo manager's advice was to hire the "best" mediocre photographer you can find. Evidently, producing an outstanding daily photo report was not as important as maintaining a peaceful status quo. Sad.

Assholes need not apply

However, if that particular photo manager was talking about not hiring prima donnas, I would agree with him totally. My philosophy was – assholes need not apply. There are too many great photographers out there who are decent human beings. Believe me, no one needs people on their staff – no matter how talented – who care only about themselves and couldn't care less about the other people on the photo staff or anyone else. Hire someone like that and you're talking about real dissension in the ranks, maybe rebellion.

Not hiring narcissistic characters doesn't mean you don't hire talented, good people who happen to be characters – as in quirky, funny, one-of-a-kind. If we followed a "hire-no-characters" rule there might be very few people in the photojournalism profession to hire, being that (it seems to me) most all of us are characters to one degree or another. And thank goodness for it.

23 THE PERFECT HIRE

The role model

Ideally, every photographer you hire will serve as a role model. But it is particularly important to bring a role model into the department when you have just taken over the leadership role. When I left the Gazette in Charleston to come to Norfolk, the Virginian-Pilot, which had long suffered under old-fashioned and uninspired management, had an immediate opening for a staff photographer. It was a staff in need of a role model.

Fortunately, I had hired the perfect photographer for this position once before.

The Bill Tiernan story

I first met Bill Tiernan soon after coming back to my hometown

---

TO THE REAR Humor, ain't it great? A little juxtaposition, two divergent species, hands on hips and there you have it. This image always gets a laugh during Bob's 1-point, 2-point show. Bill Tiernan of Charleston, the capital of West Virginia, tucked among the hills of the scenic Kanawha Valley. After 18 years of being on the road, I was back home to take the job as the morning Gazette's first graphics editor.

Bill was a photographer for the afternoon Daily Mail, whose newsroom was located across the hall from the Gazette's, in the Charleston Newspapers Joint Operating Agreement building. The competition between the two independently owned papers was fierce. In a very healthy way, the editorial staffs hated each other.

When it came to picture selection and picture use, the Daily Mail was clueless. I had been hired at the Gazette because it, too, was clueless, but had decided to do something about it. As we quickly began to turn things around at the Gazette, Bill often stopped me in the hallway with this lament: "Bob, you won't believe what the Daily Mail did to my pictures today."

Under the radar

After about a year of this, I finally said, "Bill, I don't want to hear any more complaints. You either get yourself a job at another newspaper – you're good enough to work for any paper in the country – or you come to work for the Gazette."

Having said that, I knew full well that we did not have an opening on our four-man photo staff, and furthermore, there was a strict JOA rule that forbade one Charleston newspaper from stealing employees from the other.

But then ... dreams can sometimes be the mother of invention.

"Bill, you know we don't have an opening at the Gazette, but if you quit the Daily Mail and you were standing out on the street, well, who knows ..."

When I ran the "Bill-out-of-a-job" scenario past my boss, Editor Don Marsh, his eyes lit up. He told me to run it past Publisher Ned Chilton. Chilton, not one to withhold his emotions, thundered, "By God, you're damn right we'd hire Bill Tiernan." No matter that we had no opening. This was the state's legendary Bill Tiernan, West Virginia's finest photographer.

Upon hearing the response of Marsh and Chilton, a small grin slid

SEE THE WAY BILL SEES

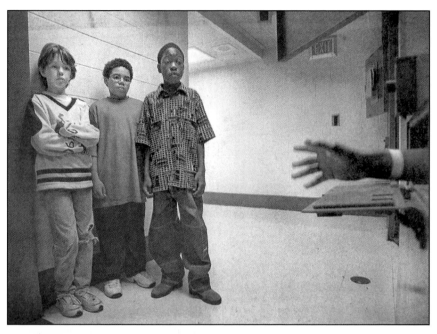

SHAKE'M UP Three boys, who have never been in trouble, get the word from a Norfolk City Jail inmate, "stay out of this place." The inmate's hand reaching out is the key to the image's success. Capturing fleeting moments like this result from the photographer keeping the camera to his eye.

COVER UP The electric chair at the Virginia State Penitentiary in Richmond, being covered up here by ex-prison warden James Mitchell, was soon to be retired. This extemporaneous moment documents that fact.

Bill Tiernan photos

across Bill's face. Two weeks later he was a staff photographer at the Gazette.

Bill hit the Gazette like a tornado. While the NPPA monthly newspaper clip contest isn't always on the mark when it comes to setting high image standards, it does reward some fine work. When Bill came to the Gazette in September, he had earned one honorable mention award during his previous eight months at the Daily Mail. During the next four months at the Gazette, with many first place clip winners, he was named regional photographer of the year.

FIRST TIME HIRE Bill Tiernan, right, was Bob's first hire at the Charleston Gazette. Later, Bob hired him two more times at The Virginian-Pilot. Bill proved to be an exceptional role model, something every staff needs. **David Vick**

Bill not only recorded superb storytelling images assignment after assignment, his professionalism was inspiration.

The perfect first hire

After reading the Bill Tiernan story above, you'll not be surprised that upon arriving at the Virginian-Pilot, and having an opening for a photographer, Bill was the first person I called. And as good fortune had it, I was able to convince him to leave his beloved West Virginia hills. His impact on the Virginian-Pilot photo report and the photo staff itself was immediate.

Bill is still the perfect role model. Not only is he one of the nation's most gifted photojournalists, recording superb images day in, day out, he is the ultimate professional journalist who leads by example. He is the pro's pro. I'm talking maturity, demeanor, dedication, passion, consideration for others, and always learning and growing.

The role model – the perfect first hire.

MIND SET Faced with the epitome of a boring assignment, Bill Tiernan unleashed his creative mind while covering a talk by Christopher Bram, author of "Father of Frankenstein." And let's give credit to that day's Pilot page designer, Julie Elman, who had the courage to run something different. **Bill Tiernan**

24 WHICH RANDY TO HIRE?

Calling all leaders

After the sad, unexpected death of Charleston Gazette staff photographer Lew Raines (Chapter Five) it was my job, as the graphics editor, to hire a photographer to replace him. It would be my first hiring search as a manager.

Even though the Gazette was a small daily, I knew that I needed to look beyond local and statewide talent. There were no more Bill Tiernans next door. I needed to look nationally. And it wasn't going to hurt any that after 18 months at the Gazette, we had built up a nice little reputation for photographic excellence.

My first move was to call leaders in the field to ask them to recommend young talent, people the Gazette could afford to pay. My first offer went to Harold Hanka, a talented young photographer from Connecticut. When his wife refused to leave New England, it was back to the drawing board.

SWEET MUSIC Photographers Randy Olson of the Charleston Gazette and Bill Ballenberg of the Philadelphia Inquirer, who took vacation to work a week at the Gazette, teamed up to produce a picture page of a Rainbow People's gathering. This lead picture captures the spirit of the event. Randy Olson

Two dandy Randys

A call to photojournalism legend Rich Clarkson, then director of photography at The Topeka Capital Journal, paid off. Clarkson recommended two young photojournalists, both named Randy, one who had graduated from the University of Missouri several years previously and one who had just graduated from the University of Kansas.

CLIMBING HIGH While at the Gazette, Bob's staff produced many full page picture stories. Bob designed all of the pages. Randy Olson

Both Randys were extremely talented and I liked them both. The Randy from Missouri, in his second professional job as the picture editor at the Coffeyville Journal in Kansas, was a good photographer, but an even better designer. And that's what I was looking for, a good shooter who could help me with the design duties at the Gazette.

But Editor Don Marsh, my strong supporter at the Gazette, could not see replacing a full-time photographer with a half photographer, half designer. So I hired the other Randy, who was the better photographer of the two. In fact he was surely the most talented young photojournalist in America coming out of college at that time.

That was Randy Olson, who, after producing outstanding work for the Gazette, went on to an illustrious career that includes becoming one of the most noted and productive photographers working for National Geographic magazine. The other Randy was Randy Cox, who went on to his own fame as a designer and visual leader at newspapers including the Hartford Courant and The Oregonian, in Portland, Ore.

The lesson: No matter how small your newspaper, when it comes to hiring, think big, think nationally.

25 LOOKING FOR POTENTIAL

No surprise images, no job

At the Virginian-Pilot, when it came to hiring photographers, we didn't look for the photographer who had the polished, winning portfolio (all the contest categories nicely covered) – photographers who may have won NPPA regional clip photographer-of-the-year awards – photographers who produced safe, good, traditional 1-point images (Chapter Seven).

We said "no thank you" to photographers who took no risks with their photography, whose images didn't jump out and surprise us. Their pictures echoed images that we had seen many times over. These photographers didn't seem to bring anything of themselves to their work. Most, it appeared, had matured early. Too early. And we sensed that they weren't going much further with their shooting.

RETREAT MOOD Most story lead pictures focus on specifics, but sometimes a story is best served when the picture is all about mood. So it is with this image about friends who have gathered at Graves Mountain Lodge in Virginia for 20 years. **Beth Bergman Nakamura**

At the Pilot we hired photographers whose portfolios were filled with 2-point, risk-taking, surprise images, or photographers whose portfolios showed great potential in that direction. The images made by those photographers with potential could be a little rough around the edges, but revealed a willingness to try new things and take creative risks.

Most of the photographers we hired at the Pilot were in their late 20s or early 30s. They had personal maturity and life experiences. They were full of passion and potential and just starting to hit their stride as photographers.

A number of them had undergraduate or graduate degrees from the top photojournalism schools in the nation – schools like Western Kentucky University, Ohio University and the University of Missouri. But not all of them. Some came from virtual obscurity. So when it comes to hiring, let me suggest that you, too, consider taking risks. To sometimes go for as yet unrealized potential.

Beth Bergman – the woman from nowhere

One of those special hires we made at the Pilot was Beth Bergman. Her story is a success story that was repeated often at the Pilot – people from nontraditional photography backgrounds fulfilling their true potential as photographers and as human beings.

As a photojournalist, Beth was the woman from nowhere. She hadn't gone to one of the famous photojournalism schools. In fact, she didn't finish college. And she had little newspaper experience, just several years on a tiny daily. What she did have was brains, street moxie, a big heart and tons of potential.

Beth was born and raised in a small Massachusetts mill town near Boston. After graduating from high school, she knocked around, taking a few college classes here and there. She was lost for the most part. She ended up in New York City, cleaned houses, was a waitress, had a few parts in off-Broadway plays. One day she asked a friend if she could borrow her point-and-shoot camera. She said that as she walked the streets of New York she "saw" pictures and felt the need to record them.

But life in the big city was tough. And expensive. So Beth left

WAITING, WAITING The story asked the question: does cartoon violence on TV have an effect on kids? When the child's hand drifted up to the TV screen, the photographer, like a cat on a mouse, knew when to pounce. **Beth Bergman Nakamura**

New York. Later, she heard about a staff photographer opening (as in a one-person staff) at a small newspaper back home. With no experience or the typical qualifications, she applied for the job. Her portfolio, so to speak, was mostly her stack of New York City snapshots. Snapshots with a distinctive artistic edge. The competition at the small daily (circulation about 18,000) was not overwhelming. She got the job.

Stop shooting those artsy-fartsy pictures

Several years later, one of our staff photographers, Michele McDonald, met Beth at a women's photojournalism conference and liked her and her work. We had a six-month temporary opening at the Pilot (staff photographer Raymond Gehman was going on temporary leave to shoot a story for National Geographic magazine). I called and arranged to meet Beth in New York City while I was on vacation. The meeting went well. I liked her. I liked what she said. I liked her pictures. Later, as we were preparing to hire her, she got a note from her boss at the small daily warning her "for the last time" to stop taking those artsy-fartsy pictures. She didn't listen. She was fired. A week later we hired this young woman from nowhere – in great part because of her wonderfully artistic, artsy-fartsy images.

For Beth, a Northeast Yankee all the way, coming to Virginia was a culture shock. Plus she was now working at a newspaper more than 10 times larger than her old paper. Until a friend talked her into attending the aforementioned women's conference she had never heard of the sponsor – the National Press Photographers Association.

Beth was more accustomed to shooting check passings than serious news. But potential doesn't necessarily come with a pedigree. When Raymond Gehman decided his future lay with National Geographic magazine, it was an outside the box no-brainer to hire this inexperienced, but special young woman to replace him.

Admittedly, we did have to teach Beth how to make sure that her wonderful images also told the story. And learn she did. From that point on, Beth Bergman became one of the truly gifted photojournalists in our profession. For 10 years she informed, impressed and delighted Virginian-Pilot readers with her original and compelling storytelling pictures.

While at the Pilot she married fellow staff photographer Motoya Nakamura. Later they moved on to The Oregonian in Portland, Oregon.

Lesson: When hiring, always look for that very special person, the one who has a unique way of seeing the world.

26 A CALL FOR HIRING DIVERSITY

Reflecting the greater community

Okay, now you know the kind of people you're searching for when hiring photographers and picture editors. But there is one more critical consideration when putting together a great photo staff – diversity of race and sex.

Hiring the best photographers and picture editors is a key to the success of your mission. But hiring the "best" goes beyond just producing great images. You owe it to your readers to accurately record the visual stories of their communities, to produce images that reach out and connect with them personally.

You do this best by having people on staff who bring different backgrounds, life experiences and sensitivities to their jobs. That

---

NEVER TOO SMALL This might not be the real United Nations, but no assignment is too small for a photographer to give it her all. With the help of body language and facial expressions the debate is over. This is a winner. **Vicki Cronis**

means a good mix of women, men and minorities – a mix that reflects the make-up of the greater community. Any photo department worth its salt cannot be a private club of any one type of human being.

What you're looking for is the best, most balanced staff possible. A staff of all white male photographers won't get it, any more than would a staff of all female Native American photographers.

Ideally, every newspaper photography department in America would be half female, half male, with minorities represented equal to their share of the population in the newspaper's region. Unfortunately this is not the way it is at most newspapers. This is not only sad; it is a disservice to their communities.

Even if a newspaper's readership is virtually all one race, that newspaper owes its readers information (visual and text) that reflects the reality of the greater world we all live in. This comes best from a diverse staff.

This was the corporate goal for The Virginian-Pilot and Landmark Communications. A visionary with a strong sense of social responsibility, CEO Frank Batten Sr. gave the order that a primary company goal was to bring diversity to the newsrooms and all other departments.

For us at the Virginian-Pilot, minority photographers made up about one quarter of our photo staff. That included African-Americans and Asian-Americans. That was pretty good. Our real struggle was increasing the number of women photographers on staff. When I came to the Pilot, there was only one woman on a staff of 18. Through the years we got that number up to three. That was not good enough.

Most American newspapers can do better. Must do better. We owe it to ourselves and to our readers.

27 HIRING A PHOTOGRAPHER

Think national search

As leader/manager of a newspaper photo operation, you have an opening for a staff photographer. The first thing to remember is that making the hire is your job. Pretty much full-time until that just right, new staff member is happily aboard.

First thought – national search. First move – get recommendations. Talk to your staff about prospects. Call your friends in the profession (hopefully they're scattered across the country). Call the photojournalism schools. Tell everyone what you're looking for – talent of course, but also good character, passion, energy and potential. (Note: I will talk more specifically about what you should look for in a photographer in Chapter 29, "The All Important References.")

SURREAL Photographers need to be encouraged to "see" differently. Raymond Gehman was a master at it. In this image, we have a surreal scene of the half hidden face of a former naval petty officer charged with spying and two TV cameramen squinting eyes to record their own images. **Raymond Gehman**

These calls should get the ball rolling with the names of some good prospects.

Ask your sources to contact those they have recommended and ask them to send you their portfolios. Of course, being the smart leader you are, you have stayed in contact with some top-notch candidates around the country. Now it's time to call them. Everyone's portfolio needs to include not only their bragging images, but also recent tear sheets (full newspaper pages) to show examples of their daily work. And I would expect each candidate to send a thoughtful cover letter (hopefully, that shows originality), plus a resume.

After making these calls, when you have received the work of enough highly qualified prospects, you might consider passing up advertising the opening. That was often the case at the Pilot. With few exceptions the caliber of applicants we received from advertising was not overwhelming and led to lots of time spent looking at work that was not as good as work already received.

Around town

It may be tempting for some managers to hire locally rather than to go to the trouble of looking nationally for the best candidate possible, someone who could make a positive impact on the daily photo report. These managers – without vision – go through their job applicant file and pick out one or two local photographers to bring in for interviews. Nice people. Maybe pretty good. And bang, that's it ... a new photographer (or picture editor) on staff.

Of course, it is possible that the best candidate, indeed, may be local, but a leader/manager will never know until they make a national search. And if the local photographer is not the best of those who could have been hired, then the photo operation, having missed a golden opportunity to improve, is the worse for it.

Another mistake is to hire the dependable, but talent-challenged freelance photographer who has been hanging around the photo department for months, or even years. The old foot-in-the-door strategy pays off for the persistent local. But if that photographer isn't the very best hire, then shame on the manager.

We were fortunate in Norfolk to always have freelancers willing to be at our beck and call. Some moved to the Hampton Roads area just for the opportunity to shoot for the Virginian-Pilot. They hung out in the department to the point that they practically became family.

But for the sake of the vision, I always told them if they had ambitions to be hired as full-time staff photographers, their portfolios and ability had to be competitive with the very best photojournalists we could attract from across the country. I made it clear that a foot in the door was not enough. I owed them that.

A manager doesn't let faithful freelancers work their hearts out with unrealistic hopes, even if it means they might stop freelancing for the newspaper. That's the chance the manager must take. It's the right thing to do.

Pigs skiing

Some newspapers insist that all hiring must go through the human resources/personnel department. Bad idea. It may be policy, but my advice is to ignore that policy as much as possible. You have got to do the searching, you have got to do the interviewing, you have got to do the HIRING. The chances of the human resources department coming up with the right candidate is about the same as a pig winning an Olympic downhill skiing gold medal.

Of course your newspaper is probably going to ask you to post your opening in-house. That's okay. But the chances of anyone in the building having the professional qualifications you're looking for is ... well ... back to that skiing pig.

Eyes on the prize

Now the portfolios (images and tear sheets) start rolling in from across the nation. Everyone in the photo department should be in on evaluating the portfolios. That means you, the photographers and the picture editors. Everyone is a part of the process. Everyone's opinion is valued. It pays off in getting the best thoughts about each portfolio. And it pays off in team building.

Making a hire really starts with a photographer's portfolio. What kind of photographer (image maker) is she or he? What kind of photojournalist (storyteller) is she or he?

The image maker: At The Virginian-Pilot we looked for images that showed the photographer had a special way of seeing the world, took risks and could make something out of nothing – as in the mighty 2-pointers. We looked for images with an artistic bent – images that surprised us.

The storyteller: Did the images visually go to the core of the story? Did they capture the mood of the situation? Did they capture the essence of the personalities (not just what they do, but who they are)?

Portfolios of the true storytellers are loaded with their own self-initiated picture stories. Picture stories are the core of what photojournalism is uniquely suited to do (see Chapter 9). No picture stories in a portfolio meant no job offer from the Virginian-Pilot.

The great one

Naturally, we always looked for greatness.

What really separates great photographers from ordinary good photographers? Great photographers consistently produce outstanding pictures from daily photo assignments that appear to have no visual potential whatsoever (which means they are shooting lots of 2-point pictures). Pretty good photographers mostly produce outstanding pictures from photo assignments that are loaded with visual possibilities. But when it comes to the routine, visually-challenged assignments (which make up the great majority of newspaper photo assignments) the pretty good photographer usually produce same ol', same ol', ho-hum, boring, cliché images.

There are thousands of newspaper photographers across the nation who assume they are at the top of their profession. But if they only produce good work from good, visually-loaded assignments, then they are kidding themselves.

Marching over the horizon

Sometimes, in my mind's eye I used to see all those job-seeking photographers marching toward me single file from over the horizon. The trouble was, for most of them – as far as their work went – the images all had a familiar, seen-that look. Like every photographer was the same height talent/creativity-wise. So my goal was to spot those photographers whose unique way of seeing the world made them rise head and shoulders above all the rest. The risk takers. The different ones. Those who had it all. The great ones.

But sometimes the great one is not out there. Then your best hire is a photographer who is still developing, but shows great potential, like Beth Bergman (see Chapter 25). Such a photographer is a better choice than a photographer who has "arrived," but whose images are predictable and don't indicate a potential for growth.

How do you spot a photographer with potential? Often their technical competence is a little rough around the edges, but you can see in their images that they take chances, which indicates they are willing to learn and grow. They usually have a non-literal, artistic way of seeing things. Frequently they have some art background.

Do you hire a specialist?

Some newspapers like to hire photographers who have a specialty, like shooting sports. But at the Pilot, we felt that the versatile photographer – one who could do it all – best served our readers. Some of our photographers were not strong sports shooters, but we felt it was more important that everyone could contribute excellent pictures to our daily news, features and business sections day in, day out. However, when it came to the big games in sports, we made sure our best sports shooters were at those games.

Inside the portfolio

Did the type of portfolio make a difference? Not to me. Good images are good images, as long as they are expertly reproduced. And the number of images didn't matter either. However, photographers who sent in loads of images (50, 75, or 100) hurt themselves because their images inevitably fell off at some point. Of course, the problem is that some photographers fall in love with all of their pictures. These photographers won't be good hires.

Portfolios that showed a number of good images, but also a number of mediocre images, always made me wonder if the photographer knew their good images from their bad images. Were the good images more a matter of random luck rather than the result of a conscious thought process? Really good photographers know their own good work. They know how to edit themselves.

I would rather see 15 great images than 30 images, some of which are great, but many of which are mediocre. At least with the 15-image portfolio I know the photographer knows the difference between good and mediocre. While I want to see a wide range of shooting subjects, not every contest category needs to be included. Photographers should only show their best images.

PERFECTION This image of Thomas Mullan hugging his daughter Kristy goodbye, as his wife Kari wipes away tears, might be a one-point picture because all of the visual elements are there for the taking. But some photographers know the precise moment to create perfection. **Raymond Gehman**

One thing I always looked for in a portfolio was captions with every image. That showed me that this photographer is a photojournalist. Plus I wanted to see the date (or approximate date) when the images were recorded. The portfolios that impressed me were the ones where most of the images were shot during the past year or so. If they ranged over, say, a five- or ten-year period, the photographer was in trouble. Most any photographer can produce some good work over that period. You're looking for the photographer who is producing lots of outstanding images NOW.

And finally – tear sheets. If a candidate works on another newspaper, I want that photographer to send tear sheets. It is one of the best ways to show what they produce in the real daily work world. The pictures don't necessarily have to be portfolio pictures, but should be darn good next-day pictures for the situation photographed.

Tear sheets get the job done

I hired Raymond Gehman because of his tear sheets.

The story: We had an opening at the Pilot. Three years out of the University of Missouri, Ray was a staff photographer at the Missoulian newspaper in Missoula, Montana. While on a family vacation back East, he stopped by the Pilot in Norfolk to show us his portfolio. It was superb, as were those of the other top candidates.

But what set Ray apart was his tear sheets, which he sent to us after returning to Montana. When the first batch arrived (a month's worth), they – by themselves – outshined some candidates' portfolios.

A week later we received 10 more tear sheets showing that week's work. They blew us away. Ray Gehman was a great hire.

28 HIRING A PICTURE EDITOR

Not an easy task

Putting together a great newspaper photo team involves more than photographers. Picture editors are the vital other half of the team. A picture editor opening is just as crucial as any photographer opening. Perhaps more so, because a picture editor is not only an editor, but also a coach, teacher, motivator and traffic cop.

Finding good picture editors isn't easy. Many don't have their personal work routinely displayed in the newspaper or on the newspaper Web site, as photographers do. So, out of sight, they're harder to find.

Of course a few do get recognized because their multi-page layouts win contests sponsored by the National Press Photographers Association and other organizations. But that certainly doesn't cover the field of qualified potential candidates.

EMOTION A river baptism is a visually loaded scene (a 1-point situation going in), but it still takes skill to capture the very peak of the emotional action, as was done here when Robin Brown was submerged in the Elizabeth River by members of the Christian Antioch Church. **Chris Tyree**

However, there is one reliable source for finding out where the good picture editors are working. Photojournalism schools. The professors will know where their star picture editor graduates are working and how they are doing. Some of these graduates will be experienced photojournalists who have been photographers and gone to college for their undergraduate degree or back to college to earn master's degrees.

Don't give me your tired

Unfortunately, at some newspapers, picture editor openings are filled without thought for the critical nature of the position. Instead of seeking a person with the special talents needed to be an effective picture editor – in the photo department and in the newsroom – some managers take the easy way out by naming a veteran photographer to the position. It is not that a veteran photographer might not make an excellent picture editor, but too often the photographer-named-picture editor is a photographer who has lost his or her enthusiasm for photography and is just putting in time.

This is not the person you want fighting for good photo assignments, for the production of great pictures and for the effective use of those pictures in your newspaper. This is not the person who will help inspire and motivate the rest of the staff to greatness.

Under your nose

Does this mean you never consider hiring a staff photographer as your new picture editor? Certainly not. While nearly all new photographers are hired from outside of the newspaper – and perhaps from the other side of the country – an excellent picture editor just might be right there under your nose.

Of the 11 picture editors I hired during my 17 years at the Virginian-Pilot, four were photographers on the Pilot staff (see footnote).

FOOTNOTE Of the seven picture editors I hired from other newspapers, one was a photographer, five were picture editors who started their careers as photographers, and one had never been a photographer, having started his career as a picture editor.

They certainly were not tired and downtrodden photographers being put out to pasture. They were bright, talented people – of all ages – who were good journalists with good news judgment, knew and loved pictures, worked well with people and all the other good stuff.

The search is on

Now that we have established that the good picture editor candidates could be either on staff or from across the country, we're ready to start the hiring process. Of course, as with the search for a photographer, we're looking for character, passion, energy, talent and potential. (Note: I will talk more about what you should look for in a picture editor in the next chapter, "The All Important References.")

If there is a photographer on staff whom you think has the makings of a good picture editor, then it is time to sit down with him or her and discuss the possibilities. If the photographer is interested, and you are convinced she or he would do an outstanding job, then perhaps the search is over.

Give that staff photographer a chance at the job on a trial basis (as discussed in Chapter 19, "The Case for Picture Editors.") Make the trial for at least three months. Hold open the photographer's shooting position. If the photographer is unhappy serving as a picture editor or fails to live up to your expectations, then he or she can return to his or her former position.

At that point start your national search. Because of the difficulty of finding good picture editors, you should probably advertise the position. Next, make contact with photojournalism schools and friends at other newspapers for the names of potential candidates. Then it is portfolio time.

Ports of call

Here is what you ask to see in a picture editor's portfolio:

- An essay describing the candidate's picture editing philosophy. It should include their views on news judgment and picture stories. The ability to articulate one's views is a must for picture editors.

- Examples of pages and Web pictures they were involved with, including information with examples that explain the following:

  > What was the candidate's rationale for selecting the pictures?

  > Why were they thought to be deserving from a news judgment standpoint?

  > What was the candidate's involvement? Include anything else that shows the candidate as a thinking photojournalist.

- If the candidate was a former newspaper photographer, include a portfolio of past photography work. Plus, include an essay on what her or his philosophy was as a shooter. Requesting essays is another way to get a feel for what kind of photojournalist she or he is. (Note: During my time at the Pilot I did not ask for essays, but it occurs to me as I write this book, that it is a good idea.)

- Also, expect a thoughtful cover letter and a well-organized resume.

Once the portfolios are in, let the competition begin.

"You are a poet!"

After years of crafting sonnets and free verse, Grace Simpson finds recognition as Virginia's poet laureate

29 CALLING ALL REFERENCES

Who are these candidates?

Whether the position to be filled is for a photographer or a picture editor, after you and the staff have looked over portfolios and chosen the candidates who have something special to offer, it is time to call references. These calls help you to gain insight into who these candidates really are.

What kind of person are they? Character? Maturity? Judgment? Work habits? Reliability? Are they high-energy, enthusiastic self-starters? Do they have a positive attitude? Are they perceptive? Do they work well with others? Do they think creatively? Are they of good heart?

Company lawyers and the human resources department say no one is supposed to speak negatively about a fellow employee. But I ask the questions anyway. The hiring stakes are too high not to.

PURE POETRY This image was the 6-column lead picture for a story about Virginia poet laureate Grace Simpson. What we have here is a risk-taking photographer and a risk-taking designer. **Vasna Wilson**

Do the references consider the candidate to be a journalist as well as a photojournalist (meaning he or she not only cares about newspaper photography, but also understands and cares about the overall newsroom mission to serve citizens)? Does he or she know what's going on in their community and the world in general? Is he or she a good listener, a good communicator? Passionate about photography? Passionate about telling stories with pictures?

It is a definite plus if the candidate attended a good photojournalism school or comes from a visually strong newspaper, or both. However, these factors are not required.

Questions, questions, questions

Photographers: Does he or she make a point to get into the newsroom? Initiate picture stories? Is he or she ethical? (Would never set up a picture to pass as an honest candid moment; would never pull any funny business with Photoshop manipulation.) When it comes to their determination to record the very best images each situation offers, are they mentally tough? (Mental toughness is a trait all the great photographers possess.) Do they write complete and accurate photo captions?

Picture editors (in the newsroom): Does the picture editor have the respect of reporters and editors? Are the picture editor's opinions sought out and listened to? Does she or he welcome the views of reporters and editors? Is he or she able to mend fences and deal with difficult personalities?

Does the candidate fight for picture use in the newsroom? Show respect for those in the newsroom even though they might totally disagree with their opinions? (What I want to know is does she or he keep their cool and not show an attitude of superiority when it comes to picture judgment, a sure way to lose debates and respect). Does she or he, in fact, win their fair share of the battles when it comes to picture use? (Keep in mind – being right is not enough, being right AND effective is what really counts.)

Does he or she have good news judgment? Understand legal and ethical issues? Initiate story ideas in news meetings? Keep an eye on upcoming news events, including sports? In other words, is the candidate a good planner? Well organized? Able to prioritize?

A problem solver? Unafraid to make decisions? Does he or she understand design and is he or she capable of offering input?

Does the candidate have the personality to meet deadlines and handle the stress of making last-minute decisions? Can he or she handle the pressure of dealing with the 24-hour news cycle?

Of course, what you are looking for in a picture editor, as mentioned above, you will welcome in any photographer you may consider hiring, as well.

Picture editors (in the photo department, the newsroom or elsewhere): Does the candidate have the respect of the photographers? Does he or she have the ability to be a good coach, teacher and motivator? Specifically, can he or she give photographers positive and constructive feedback, inspire them to perform at higher levels? Does the candidate improve photo assignments? Call photographers at home to let them know about significant changes in the use of their photos? Stress to photographers the need for complete and 100 percent accurate photo captions? Push photographers to do their own picture stories? Come up with their own picture story ideas for the photographers to shoot? Does he or she share credit for success?

Not talking

Sometimes a reference is a candidate's supervisor who knows that the candidate is applying for a job at your newspaper. This is fortunate, especially if the present boss is forthright and candid about the evaluation. But if a boss or any other reference won't say anything meaningful, there is still a way of gaining insights.

A technique that I use to get a reference to talk openly about a candidate is to ask this question: "If the candidate was to ask you, 'What is it that I need to work on to become a better photojournalist, a better staff member?' – what would your answer to them be?" I get some very interesting, helpful insights from that question.

If you're lucky, you will know other people who know the candidate. I would call them to get their opinions and thoughts. There is a good chance that you will get more objective answers from them than you will from the candidate's references, who, we can normally assume, the candidate was comfortable recommending.

And in this corner

Also, you have to learn when to act on the information you get from a reference and when not to. For instance, when I was asking Rich Clarkson about the possibility of hiring young Randy Olson, who was just about to graduate from the University of Kansas (see Chapter 24), Clarkson told me about a fight Randy had recently been in. The fight took place when Randy was shooting a Jayhawks basketball game and he and a fan got into it.

I talked to Randy about the fight. He admitted it was not his best moment. Despite the incident, I hired Randy.

Of course I could have made a different decision. I had to weigh fear of making a mistake against Randy's obvious photographic talent and Clarkson's assurance that he was a "good kid." But I felt a kid getting into a courtside fight didn't alone disqualify him from getting into the ring of photojournalism.

It was a good first for the both of us. My first hire to fill a staff opening. Randy's first full-time staff job.

Reading between the lines

There are times you need to read between the lines. Sometimes a reference will gush with glowing remarks about the candidate. Listen carefully for that one possible nagging negative. If you pick up on that one negative, it may be more meaningful than all of the positive comments put together.

Case in point: We were hiring a summer photo intern at the Virginian-Pilot. I was talking to one of our leading candidate's references, a director of photography at a paper where the candidate had interned. She went on and on about how great this kid was. Somewhere in all that positive verbiage she slipped in, "but sometimes we had to kick him out of the door to get him moving."

Despite that comment, we hired him for the summer. Big mistake. That young man turned out to be our most disappointing intern ever. His mode of operation – or more accurately, non-operation – was mostly sitting on the photo department couch, as if glued there.

I'm not saying that one negative comment should always outweigh all the other possible positive comments. Listen carefully to the less-than-positive remarks, as well as the glowing ones, then make your decision.

30 THE INTERVIEW – MAKE IT PERSONAL

Coming to town

A top candidate is arriving for the interview. You've done your homework on her and you have high hopes she could be the one for the job. She's flying in from Somewhere, USA. You've told her to either catch a cab or hop on an airport limo to come to the newspaper downtown. You'll see her in your office at 10 a.m.

Wrong.

You personally meet her at the airport.

Meeting prospects at the office may be the traditional way to start the recruiting process, but if you want to get off to the smartest start, then you – the leader of the photo operation – meet her at the airport and drive her to the newspaper. It is as much your job to

---

WHAT TO EXCLUDE Think of the cliché images you've seen taken on an assignment like this, to show an Olympic hopeful working out. By framing Alexis Brion in a sea of legs the photographer creates a strikingly uncommon image. **Tamara Voninski**

impress her, as it is her job to impress you. If she is a strong enough candidate to be flown in, then you want her to know right off that your interest in her as a job candidate is anything but routine.

Maybe you feel you're too busy to go to the airport and have asked a subordinate to pick her up. Maybe you think it is her responsibility to get herself to your newspaper because your paper is one of those big, prestigious organizations where she should feel honored just to walk through the front door and down the hallowed hallways.

If you're smart, you'll meet her at the airport.

And if you're smart, she will be scheduled to be in town for several days. At least one day for interviews and another for showing her around town.

One-on-one

Of course, you will be the first to interview her. You might show her around the photo area and the newsroom first to help her to relax and feel welcomed. Your drive together from the airport will have already helped in that regard.

The key to a good interview will be your ability to make her feel comfortable. Being the nice person you are, that shouldn't be a problem. Now it's time to go over her portfolio with her. Get to know her some, to try to find out who she is.

What is your first impression? Does she project confidence and professionalism? Is her appearance appropriate? Is she easy to talk to? Is she forthright in telling you about herself? Is she asking you good questions? Is she a good listener?

You've already talked to her references and gotten their comments about some of her strengths and, if the references were forthright, perhaps some of her weaknesses. Now it's up to you to find out how she sees herself. The questions I would ask:

- How did you get into photojournalism? (If you haven't already asked this icebreaker.)
- If we hire you, what would you hope to learn here at our newspaper? What would you hope to teach us? What would you hope to accomplish?

- Do you have interests outside of photojournalism?
- Do you read much? What do you read? Newspapers? Magazines? Books?
- What are some of the interesting experiences in your life?
- What do you see yourself doing in the future?

But no sneaky, contrived questions.

Whether she is a candidate for a photographer opening or a picture editor opening, there are many other questions you can ask her. Most of them you have already asked her references. Now it's time to get her thoughts. You ask those same questions to not only get her self-evaluation, but to emphasize to her the importance of these subjects.

If she is a photographer, when you go over her portfolio and published work, ask her to tell you about each image. How she got each one. What she was thinking. Ask her how she comes up with her own picture story ideas. (We know she has picture stories in her portfolio, because you wouldn't have brought her in if she didn't.)

If she is a picture editor, when you go over her portfolio, ask her about her involvement in each situation. Ask her if she had to convince others to run some of the pictures that went with stories. What were her arguments?

One of the critical skills necessary to be an effective picture editor is the ability to articulate why you like or don't like a picture. In the newsroom, picture editors sometimes face a no-holds-barred situation when it comes to fighting to get pictures into the newspaper. At the Pilot, to help determine the candidate's verbal skills of persuasion, we would throw down a stack of good and bad pictures, then ask the candidate to tell us why they liked or didn't like them.

Some candidates failed this simple, but tough, little test. They didn't get the job.

But for those who articulated their thoughts well, this exercise also gave us an idea of how they thought about pictures. What they considered superior images. Did they have a natural eye for and an appreciation of unique images? And the truth was, if a prospective picture editor was going to work at the Virginian-Pilot, it was important that the two of us, for the most part, shared a common vision of what constitutes good visual content.

She's interviewing you, too

And if it turns out – after you, the photo staff and other management people have talked with her – that she could be that special person with the talent, attitude and desire who could strengthen your staff and impact the photo report, then you roll out the welcome mat. Show her your town – the cool renovated downtown area, the art museum, the civic arena, the interesting places where she might like to live.

Make sure she gets an opportunity to talk with members of your photo staff. They should take her to lunch or dinner. You should be in on a meal or two yourself.

Of course she will talk with some of your paper's leading editors, starting with the managing editor or editor (whomever is in charge of the newsroom).

Encourage her to talk, one-on-one, with any of your photographers and picture editors, plus reporters and word editors. She has a right to know the kind of people she could be working with, as well as what the general atmosphere is at the paper.

Several visitors to the Virginian-Pilot told me they were surprised and delighted to hear chatter and laughter as they walked through the newsroom, especially when they thought of the heads-down, dour atmosphere at the newspaper where they worked. They concluded, rightfully, that the Pilot would be a positive and fun place to work.

Open and honest

And when the interviewing and socializing (as in recruiting) with our Somewhere, USA candidate is all said and done, it is you who drives her back to the airport to see her off.

In other words, you are letting her know that you like her and that she could well be your choice to fill the job opening. Why go to these lengths to impress this candidate? Because if you feel she could be the person to make a difference at your newspaper, you can't afford to let her get away because you held your true interest to yourself. Even though you may be interviewing one or two more candidates, you don't want to lose this excellent candidate to another organization because she wasn't fully aware that you and the others were highly impressed with her.

As the leader of the photo operation with the job of building the strongest possible photo staff, you can't afford to miss out on hiring your strongest possible candidate. Your staff is the franchise. You can't have a great staff – thus a great photo report – without great people.

On the other hand, if the candidate's interview went poorly, it's a different story. Then you are polite, but noncommittal. However, if she asks you how the interviewing went, you gently tell her the truth. Do you drive this candidate back to the airport? Yes, out of common courtesy and consideration for the time and effort she put into coming to your town.

It's always a two-way street, no matter how the interviewing goes.

31 CLOSING THE DEAL

No low-balling

It's decision time. Hiring time. You, the photo staff and a few of the editors in the newsroom have interviewed three candidates. A lot of discussion has taken place. Who will bring the greatest strengths, immediately and in the future, to this important opening?

In the end, as the leader of the photo operation, it must be your decision who to hire. And guess what? You (with a lot of input from others) have chosen the candidate interviewed in the previous chapter.

"I'm calling to let you know we want to offer you the job," are your words to her over the phone. Hopefully, you have a happy person on the other end of the line.

While you had talked pay range in general during the interview, you now make the specific offer. You may get an immediate yes to the job and pay. Or the candidate may ask for time to think about it. Either way is okay.

HEADS START Newspaper photo coverage of political campaigns produces some of the dullest images imaginable. It doesn't have to be that way, as seen here with politicians James Gilmore III, George Allen and Bob Dole at a rally in Norfolk, Va. **Huy Nguyen**

When it comes to what pay to offer a new employee, the one thing you don't want to do is try to get them for as low a salary as possible, or low-ball them. A person treated this way, even if they take the job, will, at some point, realize they've been low-balled and will resent it. Not a happy situation. And if you rationalize the low salary offer by saying you'll make it up after she has been aboard awhile, that's not really fair, and at most newspapers, it's much easier said than done.

But the candidate says "yes." Now you're both happy.

Other things to think about

What are some of the things you can do to make your new hire's transition a positive one?

- Extend all the help your company will allow for a move to your town. Give all the help you can to find a place to live, including a second trip for house-hunting. Talk to the staff and friends about good possibilities.
- Give the candidate whatever time is needed to arrive on the job. Sometimes people have particular circumstances that call for a delayed arrival. Some managers, who are hurting to fill an open slot, will demand the new hire come now or the deal is off. I was

---

ADVICE WELL TAKEN

When I took the graphic editor job at the Charleston Gazette, it was one of the best decisions I ever made. But it almost didn't happen and I learned a lesson.

Salary. One of the Gazette executives (actually a first cousin of mine) had told me the Gazette could match my Cincinnati Enquirer salary. When I finally sat down with Editor Don Marsh to accept his job offer, the salary came up several thousand dollars short. I suppose it was understandable, the Enquirer was a much larger paper than the Gazette.

But nonetheless, I sat in front of Marsh's desk in disbelief. Do I take this job or not? "But," I pointed out, "I was promised ... "

Fortunately, I recalled the words of a fellow photojournalist, Tom DeFeo, "Don't ever turn down the right job because of money." I took the job and my life was changed forever.

always willing to put up with a short staff a while longer to get the right person to come to our newspaper for the long run. How long is a long run? You hope it will be years. But in great part, how you run the photo operation and how you treat your staff will determine if talented people stay or not. The candidate isn't signing a lifetime contract.

- I have heard of newspapers that demand new hires sign contracts that stipulate they will stay a certain length of time. That's ridiculous. The working conditions and opportunities the newspaper offers its employees is what should keep them there, not a contract.

Well, there you have it. You've just hired yourself a terrific new picture editor ... or was it a photographer? No matter, you're getting the hang of this leadership/management thing.

Don't forget the other candidates

But what about the people who didn't get the job? The other two candidates you flew in? And all those other portfolios still stacked up in the corner?

Well, of course, as soon as you've confirmed your new hire, you call the other two top candidates and let them know personally how much you appreciated their interest in your newspaper. And if you would be interested in them again – if another opening occurred – let them know that. But if you wouldn't be interested, and they ask, be absolutely honest with them. Gentle, but honest.

And don't forget to return their portfolios and the portfolios from all the others who applied for the position. Let each applicant know you appreciated their interest with a personal letter of thanks.

Finally, sit back and relax a bit, and look forward to the arrival of your new hire and the new ideas and energy she'll bring to the newsroom.

32 THE FLIP SIDE OF HIRING: TIPS FOR JOB SEEKERS

(Leader/managers might also want to take a peek)

Applying for a job

Dreams can burn bright for newspaper photographers and picture editors wanting to move on to better, and perhaps bigger, newspapers. But sometimes when applying for that dream job little things can knock these hopefuls out of the running.

Many of these "little things" can send the wrong signal when it comes to submitting a portfolio, resume and cover letter. But other things can send the right signals. Following are some dos and don'ts.

A LEG UP We encouraged photographers to look for that little extra. Washington, D.C., freelancer Michelle Frankfurter had such an eye. We ran a story on Haiti she did for us on spec. This image of mourners at a funeral was one of ten pictures that ran in the Virginian-Pilot. **Michelle Frankfurter**

The photographer's portfolio

If you have a certain shooting style, let the images in your portfolio show that style. Don't try to second-guess what a prospective boss might like. If you do, you just might miss getting the job because you outguessed yourself. My advice – when it comes to showing your work, be honest about who you are as a photographer. Put in what you like, your favorites.

Photographers looking for their first newspaper job may not be able to follow this advice. But after they gain some experience, they should let their natural style of shooting speak for itself.

Don't predetermine the number of images to include in your portfolio. Don't submit weak images just to fill a particular shooting category. Don't send so many images that your work invariably falls off.

The point is, submit only your very best work, images you are truly proud of.

As discussed in Chapter 27, portfolios that show really good images along with mediocre images always make me wonder if the photographers know their good work from their bad. Were the good images more the result of luck than a conscious thought process? The really good photographers know how to edit themselves.

And show that you are doing good work NOW. Make sure a good number of your images have been recorded within the past year. Submit recent tear sheets. Also, show that you are more than a shooter. Show that you are a journalist, as well, by captioning and dating each portfolio image.

Other thoughts:

- Don't get attached to mediocre pictures even if you worked your tail off to record them. Mediocre is mediocre.
- Don't include routine pictures of famous people no matter how thrilled you were to record them. Mediocre is mediocre.

Suggestions for what to include in a picture editor's portfolio can be found in Chapter 28 under "Ports of Call."

Calls and drop-ins

I know that some photo managers don't want candidates calling them directly about a job opening or to see where they stand in a search for a new hire. It was always okay with me. While it might be annoying to some managers, for me, it showed interest and a "go-for-it" spirit.

Should you drop by a newspaper unannounced to show your portfolio? Once again, go for it. That, too, was okay with me. If you get turned down, what have you lost?

The cover letter: First impression

Don't underestimate the value of the cover letter. A good one can immediately grab the attention of the person you hope will hire you. It should be straightforward and honest. It should be original without being corny. Avoid cliché statements. Show knowledge of the newspaper.

One such letter came to the Pilot from an intern candidate attending the University of Texas. Huy Nguyen had an excellent portfolio, but his letter knocked us out. He told his story of escaping from Vietnam as a boat person when he was a young boy. That was impressive enough, but it was his superb writing ability that told us this student was special. Huy Nguyen got the internship and later a full-time staff job at the Pilot.

So a cover letter can mean a lot. With that in mind, here are some thoughts (they may seem obvious, but it is amazing the mistakes some applicants make):

- Don't send a cover letter that starts off, "Dear Director of Photography" or some such title, with no name. If you're too lazy to find out the name of the director of photography, well, your letter and portfolio immediately go into the out stack. (Most applicants who made this mistake were students applying for internships.)
- When you do address your letter to the proper person by name, make sure that name is spelled correctly. And the name of the newspaper, too. In fact, there should be no misspelled words in your letter, resume or portfolio. (Note: Not so easy for me to say. I confess to being one of the world's most creative and imaginative spellers. But I work hard to get it right.)

- Please, don't write that you are confident that you are the right person for the job. This was a typical statement I found in letters from students. I don't know who was teaching them that, but I found it to be presumptuous and annoying. Confidence has its place, but let the newspaper where you are applying decide if you are the right person for the job.

The resume

Keep your resume as short as possible. Don't list every award you ever won, just the big ones. List at least three references. As many as five is okay. List their full titles. Make sure you include their telephone numbers and e-mail addresses.

Dressing for the interview

When you go for a job interview, the way you dress makes an important first impression. Don't under-dress, like shorts or raggedy jeans. Don't overdress, like one young woman who came to my office for an interview one afternoon wearing a flashy, low-cut cocktail-type dress. I wondered – what was she thinking?

Casual, but neat, was good. For women, a dress, slacks or nice jeans were fine. For men, the same, but minus the dress. Ties weren't necessary. Personally, I always hated to wear a tie.

Jamie's persistence pays off

Don't be afraid to let a photo department leader know that you would love to work at her or his newspaper. All things being equal, I would hire the person who showed a real desire to work at my newspaper.

That's how it was with Jamie Francis. Jamie was a young photographer at the Durham (N.C.) Herald-Sun. He wanted to work for the Virginian-Pilot in the worst way. The first time he drove up to Norfolk to talk with me, I was very impressed with him as a person. Not so impressed with his portfolio. We talked about his pictures. How he could improve them.

From that point on he regularly sent me his latest clips from the Herald-Sun. And periodically he returned to Norfolk to talk to us. Each time his images were improved. In time, Jamie won North Carolina Press Photographer of the Year honors. But he still wasn't ready for the Pilot. However, he never gave up. About two years after I first met him, Jamie was ready. We had an opening. He got the job. He was an outstanding hire.

Jamie Francis went on to become one of the nation's finest photojournalists. After leaving the Pilot he worked for the The State in Columbia, S.C., the St. Petersburg Times and then at The Oregonian, in Portland, Ore.

33 DREAMS CAN COME TRUE

You never know

Many eager young photographers, hungry for knowledge, visited the Virginian-Pilot photo department looking for advice. Some unannounced. I made a point to talk with each one. For one thing, who knows? They may be that unknown talent to keep an eye on. But most of all, I hoped that I had something to offer in the way of advice that might help their ambitions come true.

Some had impressive talent. Some didn't.

It's easy enough to encourage those with obvious talent, but what advice is there for those who lack any discernible talent at all? Do you tell them to "get out of the business kid, you don't have it?"

No. For one thing, who was I (or anyone else) to cut down

THE EMOTIONAL CONNECTION This is a great 1-point picture, because it makes a powerful emotional connection with the reader. Photographers' portfolios should be half 1-pointers like this and half 2-pointers (something-from-nothing pictures). Here, Esther Yates hugs her daddy, Rodney Yates, after his return from the first Gulf War. **Denis Finley**

someone's dream tree? The truth is, you don't really know if any one individual is totally devoid of – in these cases – photographic talent. For example, military photographers stationed in Norfolk regularly freelanced for us at the Pilot. Some were talented. Others came to us with seemingly marginal ability, but after a year or so of working with and being inspired by our talented staff, these "marginal" military photographers made remarkable improvement.

Never underestimate desire and determination. Let me illustrate with four success stories:

The power of desire

She was tiny by any comparison, very young and painfully shy. It was some years ago at one of the Northern Short Course conferences. She approached me with her portfolio and, in a small, quiet voice, asked if I would look at her pictures.

One by one I went through them. By any standard, they were, to put it bluntly, awful. I told her, in the most honest but gentle way I could, what her pictures lacked. And they lacked a lot. Then I pointed out the most encouraging aspects of her images – as few as they were.

A year later at the Northern Short Course she came to me again. Once again I looked at her pictures. They weren't really good, but they were no longer awful. We talked about her progress.

The third year at the short course she was less shy than when I first met her. Once again, we went over her work. Miracle of miracles. These were real photojournalistic pictures.

Smiles all around. This determined, never-give-up young woman was happy. And I was happy for her.

By this time she had earned a staff photographer position with the Journal Tribune in Biddeford, Maine. And she was not only shooting, but also doing her own picture story layouts. Later that year, thanks in great part to her layouts, the Journal won Best Use of Photos for small newspapers in the National Press Photographers/University of Missouri Pictures of the Year competition.

Soon after that the Orange County Register in California hired her as an assignment picture editor. From there it was on to the Boston Globe as its sole newsroom picture editor, to the Providence Journal as its director of photography, and back to the Boston Globe as its multimedia editor. Today Thea Breite is recognized as one of the country's leading visual journalists.

Not bad for a kid who started out with "no talent."

You just never know.

Kick 'em into school

Not long after I returned to my home town of Charleston to take over as the morning Gazette's first graphics editor, I began seeing outstanding sports pictures being published in the Daily Mail, the Gazette's afternoon rival across the hall. I came to learn they were the work of a young freelancer named Bill Kelley III. Bill was 19 at the time. For the next year he was doing most of his freelance work for me at the Gazette.

During that year, Bill married his childhood sweetheart, Alison. The new groom's fondest desire was to be a full-time newspaper photographer. But I told him he needed to go to college, married or not. I recommended Ohio University's photojournalism program. I talked to Chuck Scott (the legendary director of the program) about Bill. He was accepted for the fall term.

Then it happened. Bill's dream was handed to him on a silver platter. The Daily Mail offered him a full-time staff photographer position. He had an agonizing choice: take a job he'd dreamed of, or go to college.

Well, Bill wasn't stupid, he went to college. He became one of OU's outstanding photojournalism students. After graduating and working for the Fredericksburg (Va.) Freelance Star and the Memphis (Tenn.) Commercial Appeal, I hired him at The Virginian-Pilot. He was very good, and not just at shooting sports. Later he was one of the Pilot photographers who switched to picture editing.

Through the years I have advised many young hopefuls and mid-career professionals to either go to college or go back to college. For those who did, almost every one of them did well in the profession. The formula – go to a good photojournalism school, learn, get connected, get a good job. Photo internships and picture editing internships are a vital part of that formula.

Internships play an important role in the next two stories.

What age barrier?

My first meeting with Bill Blanton – he was 42 at the time – took place late one night in my hotel room at a Virginia News Photographers Association conference in Richmond. My wife, Millie, was sound asleep a few feet from us. Bill, who had been a teacher at Radford College and was working as a reporter/photographer at a twice-weekly newspaper in the hills of western Virginia, sat there with his portfolio – a cardboard box stuffed with pictures of all sizes and shapes, plus his story clips.

Under the dim light of one small lamp, I looked at his photographs. His images were not sophisticated, but they had a nice feel to them. Good composition. Good human feelings. Warm. Real. This man from the mountains had talent.

Bill wanted to be a photographer at a daily newspaper. "Go to Ohio University to study photojournalism," I told him. He did, becoming – at that time – the oldest visual communications graduate student ever at the school. There, he got connected to the world of photojournalism and learned things he needed to know.

That following summer, we offered Bill a photo internship. We joked with him about "being the oldest intern in the country." After leaving OU, he landed a photographer job at the Columbus Dispatch. A few months later, we offered him a picture editing position at the Pilot. I told him that within 18 months he would be getting offers from other newspapers to head up their photo operations. It didn't take that long (good visual leaders were hard to find in those days, too).

After 11 months at the Pilot, Bill was offered the Assistant Managing Editor/Graphics position at the Knoxville News Sentinel. Then came AME/Graphics for the Milwaukee Journal-Sentinel, teaching at Marquette University (photojournalism, picture editing and design), and then – wouldn't you know it – we talked him into coming back to the Virginian-Pilot as a picture editor/designer.

Later, when the Naples Daily News asked him to come to Florida to be their Deputy Managing Editor/Presentation he couldn't resist the offer to again head up his own visual operation. His first year there, the paper won Best Use of Photos at the NPPA's Pictures of the Year competition, an honor it received several more times.

When Bill Blanton retired 12 years later he was managing editor of the Daily News.

Don't let age, or a portfolio in a funny looking cardboard box, fool you.

The pastry chef

At the age of 32, Denis Finley decided that being a pastry chef and former owner of a restaurant wasn't really what he wanted to do in life. Denis always had an interest in photography and had taught himself how to process film and print black-and-white images. He thought he could make it as a newspaper photographer, so after much soul searching and research, he headed to the University of Missouri in Columbia.

He did well at Missouri and applied for a summer internship at

---

THE USS INTERN-SHIP

Hiring good interns can pay off for both the interns and the newspaper. Of the 26 staff photographers I hired at the Pilot, seven of them had been interns at the Pilot.

We sometimes hired interns who were not the most advanced candidates, but who really deserved an internship because of their gritty efforts to produce meaningful picture stories, their desire and their potential. And sometimes we just liked their risk-taking images.

We quickly learned what interns had to offer because we threw them straight into the cold, cruel waters of reality. They were expected to shoot daily photo assignments, just like the regular staff. While there was lots of coaching, we didn't baby the interns. They learned and learned fast. Of course, hiring good interns helped. Their reward for good work was to team up with a staff photographer to shoot the famous Chincoteague wild pony pinning roundup in July.

the Pilot. I had to tell him he wasn't quite ready. Several months later, however, when we needed a photographer to fill in for Raymond Gehman (who was going on a two-month leave of absence to shoot an assignment for National Geographic), Denis jumped at the chance to fill in.

Our first impression of Denis was good. Our second impression of Denis, which came later, was even better. While finishing up his master's degree at Missouri, he asked us if he could work for the Pilot as an unpaid picture editor/designer intern. He needed it to complete his master's project.

Unpaid internship? No problem. Welcome back, Denis.

However, after Denis arrived, I worried. No pay – my gosh, the poor guy, still a student, could starve to death right there in the photo department. Fortunately, I was able to talk the Pilot into paying him the grand sum of $125 a week.

Denis hit the Pilot like a storm. He had what it takes to be a picture editor the day he walked through the door. I soon had his salary up to $385 a week, a regular intern's pay.

After he served an internship at National Geographic (an honor he earned for being named College Photographer of the Year) we grabbed Denis off the market, hiring him as a staff photographer. He was 35.

Denis was a gifted photojournalist who showed maturity and leadership from the start. Always interested in the workings of the newsroom, he proposed the new, innovative team picture editing system discussed in Chapter 21. There was only one problem. For his concept to work, we needed one more picture editor. At the time we had two newsroom picture editors, one to cover the day shift and one to cover the night shift. In Denis' scheme, we needed two daytime picture editors, plus the night person.

We had no openings, so where were we to get another picture editor? At the time we had 17 photographers on staff (10 in downtown Norfolk and seven in bureaus), each an important position in our photographic coverage. But when we looked at our needs, it became clear that the second daytime picture editor was a higher priority than a 17th photographer on staff.

And who better to be the new picture editor than Denis himself, the person who envisioned the new system in the first place, a person whose enthusiasm for it would be contagious. And it was.

That was just the beginning of Denis' editing career. From a fast start as a picture editor, he went on to be asked to take other editing positions at the Pilot. Features department editor. News editor/design team editor. Deputy managing editor/presentation.

And finally Denis Finley was named the editor and leader of The Virginian-Pilot newsroom.

Not bad for a former pastry chef who once was an unpaid picture editor/designer intern.

Your Hand on the Tiller

Leading and managing the creative team

34 LEADERSHIP AT GROUND LEVEL

Hand on the tiller

What should the leader of a newspaper photo operation be doing, be thinking – day in, day out – whether he or she is an assistant managing editor, a director of photography or whatever? Assuming this leader doesn't have daily production duties – as do picture editors – is this position really necessary?

Well, of course, we could ask the same question of many people in the newsroom with such titles as assistant managing editor for news (as in text), or night news editor, or features editor, or sports editor. But let's not digress.

How can a position be justified that many newspapers forego?

TUTU MUCH The best action can be backstage. Subjects switching gender roles and the photographer capturing the perfect moment during Westminister-Canterbury's "'Springtime Follies," tickle the funny bone. **Mort Fryman**

Let me tell you some of the things I did, day in, day out. What I was thinking, day in, day out.

I saw myself as the captain of the VISION, with my hand always firmly clasped on the tiller of the vision's course – our everyday course of producing exceptional photographs to fulfill our No.1 goal – the Great Daily Photo Report.

I viewed all of my decisions and actions as a way of keeping the vision on course. I viewed everything I did in terms of motivation and morale, which were the magic elixirs for producing the highest quality, in-depth, most meaningful daily photo report possible for our readers.

The demands for those decisions and actions seemed never ending. Using a soccer analogy, I often thought it was like lining up 50 balls across the playing field and trying to kick each one of them down the field all at the same time.

A day like any other

To offer some insight on a typical day for an assistant managing editor for graphics, here is one of my days that I recorded.

8:30: At home, pulled staff pictures (1 and 2 pointers) from that morning's Virginian-Pilot that deserved to go up on The Board in the photo department.

9:30: In the photo department, started opening mail.

9:32 to 9:52: Talked to photographer Mort Fryman about his back problems and physical therapy program.

10:00 to 10:12: Talked to photographers Bill Tiernan, Bill Kelley and Raymond Gehman, and photo department manager/assignment editor Bill "Abby" Abourjilie about the possibility of the photo desk photographer shift being divided up five ways each week.

10:12 to 1:02: Talked with photographer Bill Kelley about today's Virginian-Pilot local picture use; called John Pruitt, Suffolk Sun editor, to discuss the pregnancy series cover picture for the Sun (a Pilot neighborhood tabloid); talked to Bill Kelley about running his Alzheimer's disease story on Thursday and Friday; looked over the features department's art assignments on the Aging series; gave office secretary Mary Brantley this week's tear sheets to put up on The Board.

1:02 to 1:08: Talked to photographer Denis Finley about missed picture opportunities with stories in the paper; then talked to Bill Tiernan about the same.

1:10 to 1:13: Talked to photographer Lois Bernstein about Pictures of the Year competition and our picture use.

1:14 to 1:24: Talked with Abby about possibly covering the Atlantic Coast Conference basketball tournament with a new portable transmitter; and talked about photo assignments for downtown staff for the Aging series.

1:30 to 1:34: With Bill Tiernan, went over his pictures of the Virginia legislature in Richmond to see what else needed to be shot for the weekend story and picture package reviewing this year's legislature.

1:34 to 1:35: Looked over the corrected copy of photographer Michele McDonald's annual performance review.

1:40 to 1:50: Talked with Lois Bernstein about the quality of her assignments.

1:50 to 1:52: Called John Cornell of the Northern Short Course to talk about plane tickets to the NSC.

1:59 to 2:01: Called National Press Photographers Association president Tom Strongman to discuss POY yearbook. Left message.

2:02 to 2:35: Talked to Abby about getting hotel for ACC tourney coverage; read in-house publication, Week in Review.

2:45 to 3:24: In the newsroom, gave Michele McDonald's annual review to secretary Barbara Carraway before it was passed on to Managing Editor Jim Raper and Editor Sandy Rowe; in the art department, talked with artist Ken Wright and scheduled his annual review for Thursday at 2 p.m.; also talked with artists Sam Hundley and Mal Thornhill; stopped by features department, talked with page designer Peter Dishal about a layout and picture use; stopped by engraving to check on photographer Robie Ray's California fashion page color key (as suggested by Peter) and talked to engravers Chuck Taylor and Ray Borchert about a

Sunday section front and its poor color reproduction.

3:25 to 3:40: Back in photo department, talked with photographer Raymond Gehman about the crop of a picture on the local page of the afternoon Ledger-Star, plus other photos, and about the photo schedule; talked to photographer Denis Finley about what engraving said about the Sunday section front reproduction.

3:41 to 3:44: Read letter from Indiana University photojournalism professor about helping him decide curriculum standards for his photojournalism students.

3:45 to 3:51: Jeff Cowart of AP called to ask if I would consider leading a session about sports pictures and information graphics. I said I'd let him know Thursday.

3:52 to 3:53: Abby checked with me about two Business Weekly assignments.

3:54 to 4:01: Secretary Mary Brantley handed me records on color use on the press. I checked figures.

4:02 to 6:59: Photographer Bill Tiernan tried to talk me into buying his old car; out in the newsroom, talked with ME Jim Raper about the Ledger-Star redesign, Bill Tiernan's coverage of the legislature this week, the Weekend In Review, etc.; attended news budget meeting; talked with director of news operations George Bryant about salaries; stopped by engraving and talked to Ray Borchert about the color reproduction, comparing the color key to the tear sheet from my home delivered paper; back in photo department, looked over the Sacramento Bee newspapers (we subscribed to other good photojournalistic newspapers for ideas and inspiration); and some other last minute stuff.

7:00: Left office (no lunch); 9 1/2 hours (not counting pulling tear sheets at home). A short day.

Don't call me boss

Yes, it was true. I was in charge. I had full responsibility for the photo department, the photo report. I was the guy with the vision. Things could go down in flames or fly depending on how I handled the job. Yes, I was the head honcho. I had no doubt about that. I knew it. Everyone knew it.

But don't call me boss.

One of our photographers, a bureau chief photographer, sometimes called me "boss." The term didn't fit. Made me feel uncomfortable. "David, don't call me that." Why not? Why should I care if one of the photo staffers called me boss? I was their boss.

For me, it was a personal, emotional reaction to the term "boss," a term that through the years I had come to associate with those supervisors who were good at giving orders, but lousy at motivating the staff. I associated it with rigid, vertical, military-style command. I associated it with "had to be in control" bosses, who feared that any loss of control was a sign of weakness. Lose a little control and, maybe lose all control. I associated it with bosses who managed through fear and who, I felt, ironically, were fearful themselves.

So what did that make me? Even though I was the person in charge, the boss if you will, I thought of myself as being the coach, adviser, counselor, "we're all in this together, we're a team," head problem solver, salary-fighter for those deserving more money, voice of photo, lead blocker to clear the way for each staffer to do their job at the highest level, and most importantly – motivator.

So don't call me boss. Just call me by my first name. That's good enough.

Not about you

If you, as the photo leader/manager, are to be successful, it can't be about you – your power or fame. It has to be about doing the job and doing it right. And if you do, then success will come and, if you're lucky, maybe a little bit of fame.

And to do it right, never, never forget your staff. The success of your vision will come through the staff's success.

As the photo operation leader, don't get so hooked on learning the new technology that you forget to take care of your staff. I made the choice to not become a technological expert in order to devote my full time to working with and motivating the staffs in Charleston and Norfolk. I was willing to depend on others on staff to be the technological gurus.

And don't over-obligate yourself to seminars and workshops and the like to the point that you have to introduce yourself to your staff when you return to the newspaper.

In both scenarios above good photo leaders have lost their jobs.

Admittedly, in today's multimedia age a leader/manager must be knowledgeable about the latest technology. But to fulfill the vision of a great daily photo report – in the newspaper or on the Web – there has to be a balance. You must continue to be the staff's champion and motivator. The staff is the franchise.

Always wish them well

It is not surprising that if you build a great photo operation people will line up at your door to become a part of that greatness. That certainly happened at the Virginian-Pilot. But staff members do leave the great operations. And when they do, you want to make sure they leave for the right reasons. Like family considerations, a chance to head up their own operations, or an opportunity to work for a publication like National Geographic magazine (as did Pilot photographers Karen Kasmauski and Raymond Gehman).

But no matter why they go, when they do, you want for them what they feel is best for themselves. I learned that if you truly care about each person on your staff, the staff will care about you and your mission.

Everyone is a winner.

So you wish them well.

Other things to think about:

- Being proud of your staff's accomplishments is okay. But be sure to leave your own ego at the photo department door.
- Even when you think you have a lot of good ideas to offer in a meeting, make sure you shut up long enough to let other people express their good ideas. That's something it took me a while to learn.
- Never get yourself into the position of feeling trapped in your job. Being permanently miserable at work isn't worth it. Always have a plan of escape. Even if you have a family, be ready to take a lesser

paying job. Money isn't everything. Life is too short to willingly remain miserable.

- The road to success is to learn from the past and deal with the reality of the present, as you fight for a better future.

Come back Shane

Every day at the Virginian-Pilot, I defended, fought for and pushed the vision – in the newsroom, in the other editorial departments, in production and in the photo department. At times, other interests challenged that vision. On several occasions head picture editor Alex Burrows confessed to me his doubts about our staying the course.

"Alex, don't worry. We will win," was always my answer. "We *will* win."

My advice to any photo leader/manager is: don't be a victim. If, in the course of the day, you feel like you've been had, shake it off. Stuff happens. It's life. Don't take things personally. No recrimination. Look forward. Prevail.

Every once in a while, well-intentioned new policies came floating down from on high. If Alex and I felt a policy could hurt the photo program, we immediately went into a mad note-writing frenzy to explain to those "above" editors why the new policy should not be put into effect or should be modified. It was scary, but we always prevailed.

On those occasions, I envisioned Alex and I as the two good-guy characters in the classic cowboy movie "Shane," where Alan Ladd and Van Heflin fought the cattlemen gang in the longest barroom fight scene in movie history. At one point in the fight, Ladd and Heflin bump together back-to-back, look over their shoulders at each other with the look of "we can whip the lot of them." And they did. That was Alex and me, keepers of the vision.

Vision. Like sunlight, good things will grow and prosper from its energy.

35 WORKING WITH PHOTOGRAPHERS

Zoo redo

Not long after arriving at The Virginian-Pilot as the director of photography I was looking over the take of some pictures of the zoo in Norfolk that were scheduled to go into a story/photo spread in the Norfolk neighborhood tabloid, the Compass.

Hmmm. Not good enough.

I told photographer John Sheally, "John, you can do better than this. I want you to go back out to the zoo and give it another try."

"And I'm going with you," I told him.

I'm sure John, a veteran photographer, was a little embarrassed, but he didn't protest. I figure he was thinking it was best to go-along-to-get-along with the new boss. So off to the zoo we went.

PLEASE, NO ICE Who needs to show the ice or skates in this picture of Olympic ice skater Scott Hamilton bringing joy to cancer victim Ariana Pollock, 4? Photographers free to shoot interpretively, rather than literally, produce the most compelling work. **Bill Tiernan**

"Okay, what do you want me to shoot," asked John, I guess figuring I intended to "give him a lesson."

"I don't care what you shoot," said I. "I'm going to shoot my own pictures. I'll see you later."

SHOT HEARD AROUND THE WORLD This picture, of U.S. Army Colonel Meyer Krischer lighting the fuse on a miniature cannon during a Veteran's Day ceremony in Norfolk, was chosen best feature photo in the annual POY competition. **John Sheally**

So I went in one direction, John in another.

Later, back at the newspaper we checked over our film. John had produced five nice, storytelling images. All better than the ones he'd shot earlier. And I had come up with three decent pictures myself – pictures that I never intended to appear in print – but only to motivate.

John's five new pictures ran with the Compass story. Sometimes a person just needs a little nudge in the right direction.

A shot heard around the ...

I was often asked by the photographers to help them edit their film. Even though I was in charge, I was still flattered that they valued my opinion. One day, I again was looking over John Sheally's film. He had already printed what he felt was his best image to go along with a story about a college campus ceremony, an image of an Army Vietnam veteran in a wheelchair saluting the American flag. It was, in fact, a strong image.

But as I looked through John's negatives I blurted out, "Whoa! John, I think I've found your really best picture." It was an image of a large Army colonel down on his hands and knees lighting the wick of a miniature toy cannon to get the ceremony off with a bang.

We ran that image of the colonel and the tiny cannon as lead picture on page one the next morning. It was a wonderfully funny, incongruous picture that spoke to the most memorable moment at the event. Later in the year John entered it in the University of Missouri/National Press Photographers Association's Pictures of the Year competition. The picture was chosen as the nation's best feature picture of the year.

One has to wonder how many other winning pictures are overlooked at newspapers across America, especially at those newspapers with no picture editors or uninvolved picture editors.

In my face

One thing I learned for sure was to always be available for your staff. The open door policy never closes. And if I was screwing up, I told the staff I wanted them to walk into my office, get in my face and let me know how I was screwing up.

I was asking them for their best. They had a right to expect the same from me. What we're talking here is communications. Talking to each other, listening to each other. Letting the ideas flow. And at the Pilot sometimes it got pretty wild.

A FEW SHOOTING TIPS FOR THE YOUNG

Speaking about working with photographers, there are several tips I always passed on to young photographers:

• When shooting people close up, eliminate distracting objects from sticking out of their heads. See the background at the same time or sooner than the person's facial expressions. If you practice, you can learn to keep an eye on both at the same time.

• Except for sports situations like a baseball runner sliding into home plate, don't machine gun with your motor drive hoping that if you rip off enough shots something good will surely show up. Normally it won't. The good photographers know when the picture isn't there. They wait, wait, wait – and fire only when they see or sense something worthwhile.

• If you have a weakness in any given shooting area, then work like heck to make it one of your strengths.

One day at one of our regular staff meetings in the photo department, I was making a point. I don't remember the subject, but one of our veteran photographers, a good shooter and a good guy, begged to differ. Being of an emotional, fiery nature, his voice went up as we discussed the matter. Sometimes being of an emotional, fiery nature myself, my voice rose, too. Pretty soon it got pretty loud. Even a bit heated. Right there in front of the entire staff.

After we had made our points and settled down, I noticed the new summer intern sitting there wide-eyed, with mouth agape. He surely thought we'd gone mad. Well, maybe a little. But the fact was, we didn't get mad at each other. Why was that? Because we respected each other. He simply expressed his opinion. I expressed mine.

And that's the lesson. If you're in charge, never be afraid to let others speak up. Even loudly. You don't want people working for you who are fearful of speaking their mind. If everyone feels their opinion counts, it might get a little crazy at times, but it's healthy.

In some photo departments, woe-be-it if someone openly disagrees with the boss. Of course this is in a department where the boss is the no-nonsense "father" figure and the staffers are the children. Speak up and you're in trouble.

So you don't speak up, you don't talk back, you live in fear. And you don't communicate. Ideas don't get aired.

You just follow the rules. You don't learn, you don't grow. You just cover your ass and stay out of trouble. And guess what, the boss doesn't learn and grow either. No communication, no growth. And forget the vision of building a great photo staff and a great photo report.

Getting it, and getting it right

A Pilot photographer made a nice feature picture of schoolchildren playing on the school playground.

The problem: none of the children were identified. "There was no way I could keep track of the kids," was the excuse. "Getting names for the caption is your responsibility," was my challenge.

The solution: Track down the name of the principal; call her at home; take a copy of the picture to her home; let her identify the children. Picture runs in the newspaper the next day. Happy ending.

The point: There is almost always a way to get the necessary information for a picture caption.

And getting complete caption information is absolutely the responsibility of the photographer. That means getting the who, what, where, when, why and how, plus good quotes and any other pertinent information. No matter what it takes.

It is not the responsibility of the reporter who accompanied the photographer, as some photographers like to assume. If the reporter does help gather the photographer's caption information, and in the process gets some facts or names wrong, guess who is still responsible for the errors? That's right, the photographer.

And getting the names right is an absolute must. Some of the people we photograph may never have their name in the newspaper again in their lifetime. Getting their name spelled correctly is incredibly important. For them and for the newspaper.

"Now Mrs. Smith, how do you spell your name ... S-M-I-T-H, correct?"

"No sir, it is spelled S-M-I-T-H-E."

"Oh ... very good." Then the photographer shows Mrs. S-M-I-T-H-E how her name is written on the notepad. Same goes if the woman's name was Mrs. P-L-I-S-H-K-A, Mrs. S-T-O-R-R-I-C or Mrs. Z-I-C-K-E-F-O-O-S-E (all real names from a phone book). And then the photographer writes over top of the name "CQ" (standing for "correct" – no matter what the copy editor back at the newspaper might assume).

To be or not to be

As the photographic leader of your newspaper, you are working hard with the photo staff to inspire change. To make the photo operation one of the best in America. In so doing, does that mean anything goes when it comes to getting those great pictures?

Is that what you tell your staff? Should you and the photographers' ambitions override all other considerations? Or does your own sense of morality and that of the photographers play a part in these questions?

You bet.

Perhaps this excerpt from a story written for the NPPA News Photographer magazine by Karen Kasmauski, former Virginian-Pilot photographer and longtime National Geographic photographer, makes the point best:

> Shortly after I arrived in Uganda to cover AIDS, I walked into a room just as I heard the last gurgles of a dying baby. There was a moment of cold silence, then the mother and the grandmother started to wail. I stood there, paralyzed. I had never seen a child die. I couldn't even touch my camera. Then I started to sob. I had to sit down. I thought of Katie, the infant I left at home and my son, Will. This child was gone, no longer to be held by its loving mother. The nun escorting me didn't know what to do. I was mourning as if it was my child lying there. It took me several hours to recover enough to continue working. Over time, I saw many more children die. I couldn't take some of those pictures, dramatic though they sometimes were. I wanted to keep my humanity and preserve the dignity of sorrow for parents who suffered the unimaginable loss of their children.

> (Note: The following two paragraphs were not included in the magazine story, but they were part of Karen's original copy.)

> Years earlier, while working at The Virginian-Pilot in Norfolk, Va., I covered a car accident. An elderly driver ran into a beauty salon. A middle-age patron, her hair in curlers, had been pinned between the car and the wall. As I lifted my camera to shoot, she started wailing, "Please don't take my picture." I became that woman. I imagined a picture of myself undignified, pinned under a car with curlers in my hair. I put my camera down. She had already suffered enough pain. I couldn't see why I should cause her more by splashing her photograph across the

front page of the paper. Before I could finish that thought, I found a TV cameraman standing beside me, filming. The woman continued wailing, begging him to stop. "She really doesn't want her picture taken," I told him. His response was, "I'm just doing my job."

I eventually made a picture of firemen taking this woman out of a window on a stretcher. She wasn't identifiable. It was an acceptable picture, but not as dramatic as the one I decided not to shoot. I felt I had to tell my boss, Bob Lynn, what had happened. He was going to see the TV coverage. I knew he would wonder why I hadn't gotten the same image of the woman in curlers, crying, pinned under a car. I was sure he would be furious at me for not doing my job. Bob's reaction will always stay with me. He said, "You have to be a human being first. If taking that picture made you feel less human, then don't take it." That philosophy has guided me ever since.

36 DEALING WITH PROBLEMS

Getting tough

Great leaders treat people as they themselves would like to be treated. But that doesn't mean that sometimes you don't have to get tough.

Every staff member has his or her ups and downs. But there comes a point when the down has gone on too long, a pattern of unacceptable behavior or performance has set in. That is when you have a one-on-one, eyeball-to-eyeball talk with the staff member in question.

If you have a private office, it might take place there. Sometimes it is better to get out of the building. This has two advantages. One, it provides privacy and two, it sends a message to the staff member

FUNNY WEATHER Weather conditions produce dramatic news images, but sometimes they can also result in some delightful feature pictures. The right moment and body language in this picture prove the point. **Denis Finley**

who needs that talking to that this talk isn't business as usual.

No matter the location, the main thing is the message. And it must be delivered with straight talk. At the Pilot there was one particular photographer, who, when he put his mind to it, produced fine photographs. But his shooting was very much up and down. At his best, his images were engaging and storytelling. But, there were extended periods when they were routine and boring.

Inevitably, when we had our talks this photographer offered excuses as to why his pictures were not up to his capabilities. My response was always, "That's bullshit." Just that. No elaboration. Result: The photographer would lower his head a bit and admit he hadn't been doing his job. Post-results: Steady show of good work, at least for some months.

Turning curdled milk into sweet cream

One veteran Pilot photographer, whom I challenged with "you're capable of doing better work," told me he could produce better pictures if he received more of the good (visually rich) photo assignments. "No, that's not the answer," I said. "When you start coming back with outstanding pictures from those so-called poor assignments, like most of the other photographers do, then you'll get more of the 'good' assignments."

The truth was, the better performing photographers got more than their fair share of one kind of "bad" assignment – those highly important stories with slim visual possibilities. Why? Because they had proved time and again that they could come back with good images from these visually boring, but important stories. Thus turning curdled milk into sweet cream.

Not so impressive

Another case involved a young woman photographer, new on staff, who was using her feminine charms to impress the older male photographers. Some touchy, snuggly stuff. Nothing really over the top, but improper nonetheless. It was her way of becoming an accepted part of the staff. I talked with her. "I know you mean no harm, but your actions are unprofessional. You are a professional. Act like a professional." I never had to mention the subject to her again.

Being a peacemaker

No photo operation sails along without problems occasionally arising between staff members. When these personal conflicts occur, one of the things a leader/manager needs to learn is when to get involved and when to stay out of it and let the feuding parties settle their own differences.

Unfortunately, there are times you must jump into the middle of an emotional standoff. Some managers don't do well in these situations. They shy away from controversy, finding it easier to look the other way. Thus the sore situation festers.

But no matter your nature, sometimes you have to get involved. I personally didn't look forward to dealing with the occasional conflict in the photo department, but I knew I had to. So I would take a deep breath and plunge in.

Up the down staircase

Entire staffs have their ups and downs, too. There weren't many serious staff downs at the Virginian-Pilot, but on one such occasion the grumbling about assignments and a few other things got to the point that I took the entire staff to a restaurant overlooking a Chesapeake Bay inlet and we spent the day working on our problems. A real getaway. The idea was to gain everyone's undivided attention, to let them know that management took their complaints seriously and to let everyone have their say.

We identified the complaints and staff problems in the morning, listing them on a flip chart. Had lunch. And then during the afternoon discussed, debated and brainstormed ways to solve the problems, to make things better. Each person was given a chance to speak up. The staff came away feeling respected and listened to. The meeting had cleared the air and given everyone a feeling of a fresh, new start.

When is firing justified?

Sometimes a staffer's performance was so below her or his ability, for such a long time, that all the heart-to-heart talks did no good. There were normally two causes.

One, the individual was suffering clinical or emotional depression. In these cases the company offered the staff member professional counseling. And we patiently kept working with them.

Two, the lack of improvement was due to the individual's attitude about things at work in general and the feelings of being a victim. A tough situation indeed. But in these cases, after all the talking and trying to understand was done, then it was time for tough love.

"You can do better. You must do better. If you don't do better, you will be fired."

When a situation comes to this unhappy point, it should NOT be because you, as the leader, are asking a staff member to perform at a level beyond their ability.

For instance, in the case of the photographers, I never expected all of them to measure up to one grand standard of photographic excellence. This has become a modern day practice that I see as unfair to many older, but hard-working photographers. And totally unfair if it is used as an excuse to fire someone. What I asked of each member of the staff was for them to perform at the very highest level of their capabilities. To work hard, to do their best every day.

When it comes to justification for firing someone, you can talk all you want to about today's demanding, competitive market, and claim that if older, longtime employees can't meet the new performance standards, then firing them from the job is justified. But as far as I'm concerned, this practice is indefensible, unjust and immoral.

Faithless to the faithful

If an employee has worked faithfully for a company for many years and, when hired, fully met the standards of that day, is it okay for the company to fire that employee when his or her best work does not meet today's "new" standards? I think that under certain circumstances, it might be impossible to keep them in their old job, but, in my opinion, it is the company's ethical responsibility to find this employee another job elsewhere in the company.

Let me be clear here. I am not saying that it can't ever be justified to fire someone who has proved to be a weak performer, even if the employee is doing his or her best. I could go along with that up to a point. It would depend on how long the staff member had worked at the newspaper and their age. If the staffer had worked, say, at the paper for 6 years and was 34 years old, maybe I could see firing him or her, making sure I gave the person enough time to find another job. And that's the point, he or she would be young enough to find another job.

But when you do the same to an employee who has been at the newspaper for 28 years and is 53 years old, that is entirely a different matter. What are the chances of this presumably faithful, hard-working employee getting a decent job elsewhere? If a manager just cuts the worker loose on the sea of unemployment and says, "Sorry about that old buddy, we owe you nothing?" – then I say shame on you and shame on the company you work for.

"You're fired" – the worst case scenario

I was involved in one firing during my 20-year management career. It was a classic case of the older employee – doing his best – not meeting the new Virginian-Pilot standards of the day. The paper's editor, using the "today's competitive market" argument, wanted to fire this person, an artist (for many years I oversaw the Pilot's art department).

I argued against this impending action. And argued. Finally higher-up editors left me out of the process. They had a series of talks with the artist about his performance, putting everything into place for his firing. When the time came, even though I was the artist's supervisor, they said if I didn't want to personally deliver the message, someone else would do it. I felt it was my responsibility. I did it.

It took place early one morning in the Pilot's nearly dark, empty newsroom. The artist was at a computer designing covers for our suburban sections. I gently told him the news he knew was coming. His face was stoic. There were tears. They were not his.

Sometimes life sucks for everyone.

37 THE WAYS OF MOTIVATION

Spinning wheel of good fortune

Motivation leads to superior photographic content, which leads to more motivation, which leads to more superior photographic content and on and on … and up and up. It could be called the Motivational Wheel of Visual Good Fortune. At the Pilot we did everything possible to keep that wheel spinning.

The goal was to create an atmosphere of photojournalistic excellence through trust, inclusion, creativity, hard work and fun – to help everyone become the very best they could be. We encouraged photographers to get into the newsroom to find out what was going on, in general, and also to talk to page designers about their pictures. We included photographers in on story planning. We gave them enough time in the field to produce their very best work. We gave them the responsibility to do their own picture stories. We shifted work schedules to make that possible.

The picture editors and I encouraged the photographers to take

WHERE THERE'S A WILL The impossible assignment: juvenile offenders (you can't show their faces) being counseled. But with a little help from above, we have a minor miracle. **Vicki Cronis**

risks with their shooting, to go to the visual edge. We knew they would fail at times. That was okay. If they succeeded in coming up with fresh, compelling pictures nearly all of the time and not coming back with anything occasionally, that was better than shooting mediocre pictures ALL of the time, but fresh, compelling pictures never.

And we gave photographers the personal control of toning their own pictures to let them know we trusted their esthetic and technical capabilities. Digital technicians just did fine tuning before a picture went to press.

Motivation plus

There are many other things that you can do as leader of a photo operation to keep motivation at a high level:

- Celebrate successes, such as a picture editor working especially hard on a photo project, or a photographer going all year without one caption error. Take the unsung heroes to lunch, give out movie passes, dinner-for-two coupons, T-shirts, or whatever fits the deed. (To help us bond together, every year the Virginian-Pilot chipped in several hundred dollars to provide extra food and drink for "Bob and Millie's" Christmas potluck party at our home.)
- Make sure the photographers' monthly, rotating photo schedule is not only covering the newspaper's needs, but as much as possible is being considerate of the photographers' family needs. I spent hours laboring over new photo schedules. For example, the shifts for the 10 downtown photographers typically included three weekends-off shifts, and six shifts that were either Friday-Saturday off or Sunday-Monday off. Plus every three months the schedule was arranged so that each photographer got a "bonus" four-day weekend off – Friday through Monday. The only "bad" shift was a Wednesday-Thursday off shift.
- Keep track of the good out-of-town assignments in order to spread them around to the staff as fairly as possible. But keep in mind that the importance of some stories will dictate your choice of photographers.
- To be fair in a photographer's annual review, make sure you look over his or her entire year's worth of work. At the Virginian-Pilot, each photographer's published work was pulled every week and

put into a personal folder. Before the annual review I separated each picture into four categories – great, good, fair and not acceptable for that photographer's skill level. This was much better than simply trying to recall the images shot during the past year, certainly a dubious approach.

- If a photographer has been underperforming, make sure you have been discussing their performance with them all year long. No surprises. No criticism coming out of the blue. Totally not fair to the photographer. Also, it would mean you haven't been doing your job as a leader.
- Keep group communications alive and well. Hold regular staff meetings. Make sure everyone has an opportunity to speak up. I made a point to go around the room and ask each individual if there was anything they would like to say or have discussed. This brought forth thoughts from staffers who might not otherwise have spoken up.
- Don't try to do it all. Trust your picture editors. Delegate as much responsibility to them as is fair. It will help them grow and build their confidence. (The Pilot's senior picture editors, besides their daily responsibilities, helped me by doing some of the photographers' annual performance reviews.)
- When you are on vacation, trust the staff to keep things going smoothly in your absence. Don't be calling in to check on things. (And, by the way, relaxing and enjoying yourself on vacation – getting away from it all – is a good thing for you, too.)
- We figured that no matter how visually challenging an assignment was, 98 percent of the time the photographer should still come back with a good picture. However, when they came back and said, "There was nothing to shoot," it was okay. We believed them and I was willing to back them up.
- After my first few years at the Pilot, requests to cruise for enterprise feature pictures were out. Cheers from the photo staff.

Keep the pot boiling

There were things we did at the Pilot to keep us all in touch with our professional world and the outside world, plus let the staff know we valued them as professionals and wanted to help them grow. Many newspapers today are abandoning such practices. But this is not smart, especially cutbacks in training. Here are some of the things we did:

- Sent staff members to special training sessions and brought experts to the Pilot to teach in-house.
- Paid for staff membership in professional photojournalism organizations (state and national), and paid for them to take part in the organization's photo competitions.
- Sent photographers and picture editors on company time to state and national seminars and workshops. We sent as many staff members as possible to the Virginia News Photographers annual meeting, hiring freelance photographers to fill in.
- Subscribed to visually successful publications – newspapers and magazines – to learn from their best examples. This can and should be done, at the least by viewing such work on the Web.

Best friends

Conventional wisdom says that bosses can't be close friends with the staff. Not good form. Looks bad. For sure to cause problems.

Baloney. What does conventional wisdom know?

Some of my best friends are Virginian-Pilot photographers and picture editors. They were best friends when they worked for me. They are best friends now that I am retired. People I dearly love. To deprive me and my wife, Millie, of those friendships would have been too high a price to pay.

Did those friendships compromise our professional relationships? Not as far as I was concerned. I never gave any of my photographer or picture editor friends any special breaks. Maybe that was easy, because I tried to give everyone on my staff every possible break.

38 THE MONEY GAME

Here he comes again

George Bryant, director of news operations, was one of the key people in determining the pay of staff members at the Virginian-Pilot. A key man indeed, especially since we were a nonunion newspaper and compensation was not set by contract.

When George saw me coming into his newsroom office, which I often did, he surely thought, "Oh no, here comes Lynn again." It was always about money. But we always found time to talk about sailing. George loved to talk about his sailboat. Making friends in the newsroom is important.

When I arrived in Norfolk, photographers' salaries did not match those of reporters. In time – after many visits to George's office – photographers pay, on average, matched or was higher than that of reporters. And several photographers made more

WATERY TAKEOFF There is no reason that newspapers can't sometimes offer readers just plain pretty images, like this scene of a pelican taking off from Kinnakeet Harbor in Avon, N.C., as a cousin avian looks on. Chris Curry

money than some picture editors and word editors. Excellence in the photo department finally became a recognized fact.

Because we were nonunion, every photographer and picture editor was not paid the same. The system worked this way: The editor, the managing editor and George Bryant set the pay increases for each staff member. Middle managers like myself were not a part of this brain trust, which in my opinion was a mistake. I often disagreed with the big three's pay raise recommendations for individuals.

To rectify this, I came up with a countermeasure. I added together all the pay increases to come up with an overall pot for photo department pay increases. Once I had that total, I personally figured how the money should be distributed to each photographer and picture editor. For example, I would give top performers larger raises than upper management had approved and offer smaller raises to some average performing photographers, always keeping the money pot even.

The aim: To reward excellence, to reward those who were making the strongest impact on our daily photo report.

I mostly worked through George Bryant. If I could convince George that a photographer deserved more money than had been initially scheduled, I almost always got the money. And when the top performers know that you fight to get them more money than the budgeted amount, motivation rides high. Onward and upward.

More budgeting fun and games

I also had to manage the capital budget and the operating budget. More fun and games for Bill "Abby" Abourjilie, the photo department manager and assignment editor, and myself. My first year at the Virginian-Pilot we were told we could buy anything we wanted for the staff with the previously budgeted (before I came on the job) $500. I had to laugh. We put in a request for $5,000. $3,500 was approved. And so it went – up, up and away, year after year. Eventually the requests got into the $50,000 range.

When it came to what the department needed, Abby was indispensable. He knew all the ins and outs of the budget game. We would put in a budget, shooting for the moon, knowing we would settle for a more earthly amount, a sum that would still move the photo operation forward. Photo won and the powers-to-be felt they had done their job of trimming our request. A little psychology here, a little psychology there. Everyone happy.

Abby, a man with a heart as big as he was, was always there to make sure that the staff was taken care of: Equipment (cameras, lighting gear, computers, scanners), a fair assignment load, time off when needed. No one was going to take unfair advantage of the photographers.

Smart money

When it came to selling staff photographs already published in the Pilot we had two policies. The money for those sold to readers went entirely to the company. The money for those sold to national magazines and newspapers went entirely to the photographers.

There was good reason for this magazine policy. It was one small, but positive way to help keep our photographers from being lured away from the mid-sized Virginian-Pilot by higher-paying metro giants. That extra money – helping to keep a great staff intact – meant a lot more to the Pilot's goal of superior editorial content than if it had been sucked up by the company's general fund.

And the winner is ...

The Virginian-Pilot photographers, picture editors and page designers won many national and state awards through the years. Taking part in these contests may seem a self-indulgent exercise in ego stroking, but it isn't. One of the secrets to our success in getting upper management's approval for good pay raises and more money for equipment and travel was winning those state and national awards.

This recognition gave us a stamp of legitimacy from an outside authority, plus in-house respect for the department. Actually, when you think about requests for equipment, upper management really doesn't know that much about how the photo department works and what its true needs are. So from a psychological standpoint, the outside recognition allows upper management to give itself permission to approve money in an area in which it is not expert. This earned permission also helps when it comes to salary and travel budget requests.

What do you mean ... ZERO?

And then there was management's budget for my salary. From the start, the Virginian-Pilot was generous in rewarding me monetarily. I did good for the newspaper, it did good by me. But a few years before I retired, management decided that I was making too much money as an assistant managing editor. In fact, more than several managing editors.

I'll never forget the scene when my boss, Nelson Brown, one of the managing editors, informed me that my salary increase for the coming year would be zero, despite the fact that the photo department had had another outstanding year.

Well, I went a little ballistic. "What the hell do you mean I get ZERO? Do you know what that tells me? It tells me the company couldn't care less about the photo department and my performance – if I stay at this paper or leave! ZERO???"

At this point, I'm literally in Nelson's face. Shouting! Nelson was a good guy and a good boss. He was simply relaying the message from on high. He was sitting in his swivel chair and I, with my face close to his, went on making my heated point. As I got my face closer and closer to his, he began to bend over ... farther and farther backward. It had to be a funny scene and as upset as I was, I almost had to laugh at the time.

Thank goodness Nelson was calm, tolerant and understanding, or I might have been out of any salary at all. Well, the upshot of it was, I went on to get into the face of the paper's editor (but not to a bending-over degree). Finally management conceded to something more than a ZERO. They made it $12 a week, or less than a 1 percent raise.

But at least it was a raise. And I still had a job.

39 WORKING WITH PRODUCTION

That's you

A key part of your job as leader of the newspaper's photo operation is to work closely with the production department. You cannot concentrate on picture content and picture use, and then ignore how pictures are finally reproduced in print and on the web.

Generally, the biggest issues involve print reproduction because so many people have to do their jobs well to make the paper look good. Out-of-register color pictures surely are one of the great visual insults to our readers. One can only imagine what they must think looking at the confusing jumble of colors: "Does this newspaper know what it's doing? Why am I paying for this product?"

And they are being ill-served when they see washed out, pastel colors that destroy the mood of a picture, or when they see black and white pictures that lay weakly on the page, flat and muddy.

1-POINT GEM All environmental portraits, since they are controlled by the photographer, should be well done as is this dramatic portrait of cowboy Buck Ford. **Rob Kinmonth**

These problems can be avoided to a great degree. But it takes someone from the editorial side of the newspaper to work closely with the production department – imaging technicians, plate making and the press crews – to help form an alliance.

And that person needs to be you.

To dot or not to dot

Soon after I arrived at the Virginian-Pilot, Executive Editor Frank Caperton named me chairman of the paper's picture reproduction committee. The first thing I had to do was convince the engravers that lightening up the color images in order to see details in the dark areas was not a good idea. It was destroying the mood, thus the strength of the photographs, not to mention the morale of the photographers who worked hard to create that mood.

One of the biggest challenges was getting black and white reproduction on track. The engravers talked about getting the right amount of "dots" in all of the tones – the shadow, the highlight and the middle tones. Unfortunately, their "dot count" resulted in flat pictures on the page. No contrast. No pop.

Showing them examples of good black and white reproduction in other newspapers (rich blacks, crisp middle tones and nearly pure whites), I diplomatically made the point that dot count was not what was important, it was how pictures reproduced on the page. They agreed. The result? Good black and white reproduction became the norm.

This was an example of what could be accomplished when editorial and production worked closely together, when both understand their common goals. Good color tone reproduction also resulted from this kind of cooperation.

Engravers join photo

A few years before I retired, most of the engravers from the old engraving department were transferred into the photo department, where they became computer-imaging specialists. They loved being a part of the photo department with its friendly, open atmosphere. Quite a contrast to their previous strictly-business production world.

And having imaging specialists in the department meant photographers could work closely with them to get the results the photographers were looking for on the presses.

Registering a problem

Through the years, out-of-register color was our biggest problem. Initially, our complaints were challenged because we used out-of-register early run editions of the Pilot as examples. The press department pointed out those early run papers were so few in number that they were all but impossible to get in register.

From that point on I had three papers delivered to my house each morning, two were paid for by the company, so I could check the color registration. The idea of two extra home-delivered papers was to have examples from both our "A" press and "B" press. The papers came off of the two presses in alternate order, thus stacked in alternate order on the pickup dock. The people who delivered the papers to my home agreed to always give me two papers that were in sequence – A and B.

When one or both of my home delivered papers were out-of-register I had proof that customers in my home area also had out-of-register papers. I regularly sent the examples – good and bad – to production's quality control manager. Registration improved. Cooperation again proved itself, serving all concerned.

Thunder of the presses

Throughout my 17 years at the Virginian-Pilot I made many visits to our printing plant, which was located in Virginia Beach, eight miles from the downtown Norfolk office. Any time we had special photo stories running, I was there. I became good friends with the pressroom workers. We worked together on registration and color reproduction. They seemed to appreciate my interest and I certainly appreciated their conscientiousness and commitment to quality work.

Their attitude was always, "What can we do to help?" Professional, dedicated people can work together for the good of everyone – especially the readers.

For me, it was a thrill just hearing those big presses crank up and begin to whirl faster and faster, roaring thunderously until they shook the entire building. Watching the printed product rolling off the presses gave me a sense of completion, accomplishment. I could touch the final result of so much teamwork.

Many times I left the printing plant long after midnight.

40 THE FAMILY

The real priority

I loved the newspaper profession. I loved feeling a part of something that in its own cantankerous way helps America be a better country. I loved going to work. Didn't mind the long hours. Loved the people I worked with. Well, most of them.

But there was one thing more important than photojournalism. Family. I'm going to tell you a little about my family because I feel that if you have a family and you have the desire, energy and determination to make your family your real priority, you can do it and still fulfill your professional dreams.

For many in our hectic profession it isn't that way. A sense of abandonment on the part of spouses and children is out there. Which often leads to divorce. Lack of time with the family is a killer. But I found it doesn't have to be that way.

MEMORIES Bob, Millie and their kids, Matt, Kelly and Shannon, share lots of warm memories of the past 40 some years. Many visits to North Carolina's Outer Banks are a part of those memories. **June Morgan, family friend**

My wife, Millie, stayed home 12 years in order to be with our kids when they were young. Our children are Kelly, Matt and Shannon. They always came first. Because Millie wasn't working, sometimes that meant that finances were tight. But parenting was more important to us than material gain. I can remember when we were living in Charleston, we needed new curtains for the living room. There wasn't enough money. Going out to dinner was out of the question. The one time in three years we did go out on our own – it was our 25th wedding anniversary – we had to borrow $25 from my dad.

And even though I worked long hours as a photographer and student in Cincinnati (I spent seven years earning my master's degree while working full time), and longer hours as the photo leader in Charleston and Norfolk – if there was a PTA meeting, I was there. If there was a recital, I was there. If there was a ball game, I was there.

Through the years, I coached Matt in baseball and Shannon in softball for a dozen summers. If I had to get to work at 4:30 or 5:00 in the morning in order to make a team practice or a game later that afternoon, that's what I did. When Matt and Shannon were older, they played softball with Millie and me on a Sunday co-ed league softball team. On one occasion, a Lynn was at bat with the bases loaded with Lynns.

I worked hard five days a week, but with few exceptions, weekends were for the family. When Shannon and Matt weren't playing ball, or Kelly wasn't doing ballet, the family headed for the woods to tent camp. It was fun and it was cheap. Trips to state parks and national forests, and fly-in whitewater canoe adventures into Canada's Ontario wilderness with friends helped shape the kids' values and outlook on life. Family bonding. Wonderful memories to this day.

And Millie and I are both proud to say that our "kids" all earned master's degrees and are doing well in their professions. Four grandchildren are the cherry on top.

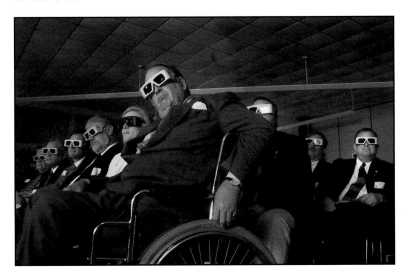

FULFILLING THE VISION

The newspaper profession has always faced problems and challenges, but its best hope to fulfill its true photographic potential is by the mantle of leadership being taken up by individuals who really know what success is and how to achieve it.

And that's where you come in.

I hope that by reading this book you have learned what it takes to be an outstanding photo leader and manager. And what it takes to build a great photo staff that will produce exceptional work every day.

FUTURE LOOK At a ground breaking for Old Dominion University's futuristic magnetically levitated train project, 3-D glasses, one "show me" face and shooting from just the right angle add up to a humorous and thematic image. **Bill Tiernan**

I have shared with you many of my thoughts and actions that I feel helped me succeed in Charleston and Norfolk. I hope you have learned that success starts with a vision to build a great photo staff and a great daily photo report. And it starts with you having the courage to believe in yourself, which will give you the courage to believe in others.

Beyond your wildest dreams

My goal for the Virginian-Pilot was to build a culture of photographic excellence so strong that it would endure no matter who the different editors were. A culture that would endure because everyone at the newspaper accepted the on-going tradition of excellence, an unquestioned given; just as the great writing newspapers accept their excellence in reporting and writing as tradition and an unquestioned given.

My fondest wish for you is that this book has given you the insight and courage to succeed as a leader and manager far beyond your wildest dreams.

Go with vision, courage and good heart.

PICTURE PAGES

The challenge

Because of the importance of picture stories, their effective presentation on a page is vital. Producing a successful picture page is one of the most difficult challenges a page designer faces. And to produce a page that everyone – designer, picture editor and photographer – is happy with is an added challenge. But it can be done.

The following section on how to design a successful picture

THE THROWDOWN Bob and staffers Lawrence Jackson, Norm Shafer, Vicki Cronis and Huy Nguyen edit down Vicki's pictures for a major story/picture spread. Such throw downs were routine at the Pilot, where teamwork was part of the culture. **Beth Bergman Nakamura**

page is taken from handout at The Kalish Visual Editing Workshop. It is the composite thoughts of Randy Cox, John Rumbach, J. Bruce Baumann, Eric Strachan, Mark Edelson and myself.

The art of designing a picture page

Know the story: If you don't know the point of the story, you can't make a good edit of the photos, and without a good edit you can't produce a good page. Talk with the writer. If the story is already written, read it. Talk with the photographer. Get his or her ideas. If the photographer has some layout ideas, listen and consider them.

Picture content is primary: The most beautifully designed "picture page" won't mean much if the content of the pictures fails the story. So you want to look for pictures that visually present the essence of the story. It can be about personality, place, what happened, mood/spirit or a combination of these and many other things.

Remember, while the term "picture story" generally refers to one story and multiple pictures on a single page, few are true stories – with a beginning, middle and end. Some pages will fall into the category of photo essay. That's okay. Don't force pictures into a preconceived "story" format. Let the pictures "speak" in their most natural manner.

The "Throw Down:" Start out by making a loose edit to allow yourself to consider different story/essay presentation possibilities. Most successful picture pages present four to five pictures on the page. One effective way to get down to the right number is to do an old-fashioned "throw down." That is, make paper printouts of every picture that might compete for a place on the page (this could be a dozen or more, etc.) and spread them out on the floor.

Start grouping pictures with similar content. As you consider each picture, your first task is to determine the "lead" picture. Virtually all successful picture pages have one picture that visually dominates the page. This picture should be the most compelling, the one that best defines the essence of the story.

Next, select a second image to run as your "second dominant" picture. This picture will normally run approximately two-thirds the size of the lead dominant picture. (Note: if you study success-ful picture pages, you will find that the overwhelming majority of them engage a second dominant picture. The page that normally doesn't work as well is one with a dominant picture played off of other much smaller pictures.)

Rough Sketches: Actually, because you may have several candi-dates for the lead picture and other pictures, it is a good idea to produce several rough design concepts, either on a computer or the old- fashioned way – pencil sketches on paper. Try different pictures in different arrangements.

Now to the page: Finally, when creating the final layout keep these things in mind:

- Use a grid (not necessarily your paper's standard grid). Every design is almost always better if based on some kind of a background grid.
- Each picture on the page needs to make its own individual content and visual statement (pictures that "say" the same thing result in what might be called "visual hiccups"); look for pictures that present a variety of visual perspectives: overall scene setter, medium range shots and close-up; look for pictures that contrast, yet complement each other; look for pictures with different perspectives (quiet moments versus energetic moments; clean pictures versus more complex pictures).
- Group the pictures. The dominant and second dominant pictures, plus the other smaller pictures, will normally present themselves best when they are arranged in a cluster-like manner. In running the smaller support pictures, make sure they are large enough to visually "read." (Note: Small "detail" pictures can work well away from the main cluster of pictures, working them in with headlines or text.)
- Most picture stories tell people stories. When selecting pictures for these stories, look for pictures that tell the reader "who" the people are, not just "what they do." Also, you don't need to see someone's face in every picture; a silhouette or shot from behind will break up what could otherwise become a monotonous grouping of pictures.
- When doing a story on one individual, look for a picture that shows that person's face up-close-and-personal. This will serve two purposes: One, it can help the reader get an insightful look

at the person; and two, it can serve as a nice contrast with other more minutely detailed pictures on the page. (Note: Encourage photographers to go after these tight, personality-telling portraits; many of these kinds of picture pages fail because all of the "face" pictures run too small to reveal a person's personality or character.)

Sometimes best is not good enough: Be aware that pictures that are individually the strongest are not necessarily the most effective when run together. This is one of the more painful challenges you'll face, because often some good pictures must be discarded to make the whole greater than the sum of its parts. Also, keep in mind that a decision to run one less picture (keeping it simple) is often the secret to success. It may mean leaving out a "favorite" strong picture, but in the end the reader is better served.

Having both vertical and horizontal pictures to work with will generally make it easier to build an interesting page. Don't choose pictures simply for their shape, but keep shape in mind. If a vertical picture contains somewhat less information than a horizontal one, but allows you to build a far more arresting page, then using it makes it more likely that readers will be drawn into the story.

If you are telling a linear story, most likely you'll want the introductory pictures at the top of the page and the ending shot at the bottom. Even if the story is nonlinear, picture placement should establish a natural flow by content and direction around the page.

Other picture details: Cropping. Crop for impact. Emphasize the natural horizontal or vertical strength of the picture. But don't crop tight for the sake of cropping. Some pictures need "space" to convey mood, sense of place, etc.

Borders on pictures. Pictures need them. Hairline or one-point borders generally look best, even for color pictures.

Details beyond the pictures: Pictures, headlines, captions and story text need to work in harmonious composition. Make sure the headline is large enough to visually "carry" the page. Always use a secondary headline (overhead, drop head, etc.) somewhere on the page. This headline should have "hooks" in it to help pull the reader into the page, but should not give away ironic surprises in the story.

Make sure the tone of the headlines – both the words and typeface – matches the content and mood of the story.

White space: There is a great deal of space on a page. There is no need to completely fill it up with pictures and text. Use white space. Use it carefully but liberally. (Note: picture pages can be done with or without a page rule around the outside of the page; when using liberal white space, a border works best).

The white space, in general, should look "balanced" (for example, if the upper left hand corner of the layout has a certain amount of white space, a somewhat similar amount might work well in the lower right corner).

Warning: Don't trap white space (where white space is surrounded on all four sides by pictures, graphics or type), thus resulting in the elements looking as if they are blowing apart (the "hand grenade" layout). White space should bleed away from the images and type.

Keep space between the elements consistent. Spacing between the page's outside box rule and the inside elements will vary. Avoid having generous amounts of white space between the page's outside box and some inside elements and then "squeezing" other elements too close to the outside box. Result: visual tackiness.

The soft-edged layout: Normally, the most successful layouts are those where white space allows for indented space between some elements (pictures, headlines and text). When the edges of three or more pictures line up, those common visual lines take on a distracting graphic strength of their own, thus taking away from the graphic content of the pictures themselves. This "soft-edged" approach gives each picture the best chance to express its own graphic "voice."

Another trap occurs when you arrange three pictures so that their common borders visually "stair step," which also can take away from picture content.

Sweat the details: Finally, be aware that your attention to the last 5 percent of detail can be the difference between an "okay" picture page layout and an "outstanding" page layout. [Note: At the Pilot, it was never "just get the page out." Designers were given whatever time needed (all day or more) to design sophisticated, compelling pages that would capture the eye of the reader.]

It ain't science: And perhaps the most important thing of all to keep in mind in designing a successful picture page: it is not a matter of mathematics or hard and fast rules, but a matter of visual and storytelling sensitivity. Laying out a broadsheet picture page is not a science, it is an art. So use your imagination. Take chances. And have fun.